Product Development & Direction: Chad Bennett, Dave Broome, Cindy Chang, Mark Koops, Kim Niemi

Project Coordinator: Neysa Gordon

NBCU, Reveille, and 25/7 Productions would like to thank the many people who gave their time and energy to this project:

3Ball Productions, Stephen Andrade, Nancy N. Bailey, Sean Bangert, *The Biggest Loser* contestants, Scot Chastain, Elayne Cilic, Tami Booth Corwin, Dr. Michael Dansinger, Lisa Dolin, Milissa Douponce, Kat Elmore, John Farrell, Dawn Fiore, Cheryl Forberg, Kurt B. Ford, Jeff Gaspin, Chris Gaugler, Jennifer Giandomenico, Linda Gilbert, Kristen Goble, Beth Goss, Marc Graboff, Erica Gruen, Bob Harper, Heather Halloway, Kim Hedland, Dr. Robert Huizenga, Frederick Huntsberry, Helen Jorda, Allison Kaz, Jessica Kirby, Laura Kuhn, Beth Lamb, Roni Lubliner, Kim Lyons, Vince Manze, Rebecca Marks, John Miller, Kam Naderi, Todd Nelson, Jennifer O'Connell, Carole Panick, Joanne Park, Trae Patton, Liz Perl, Jerry Petry, Craig Plestis, Kevin Reilly, Chris Rhoads, Lindsay Rickel, Beth Roberts, J. D. Roth, Lauren Santiago, Leslie Schneider, Ben Silverman, Charles Steenveld, Lee Straus, Amy Super, Deborah Thomas, Matt Vassallo, Brian Wendel, Bob Wright, Yong Yam, Jeff Zucker

COOKBOOK

NBC

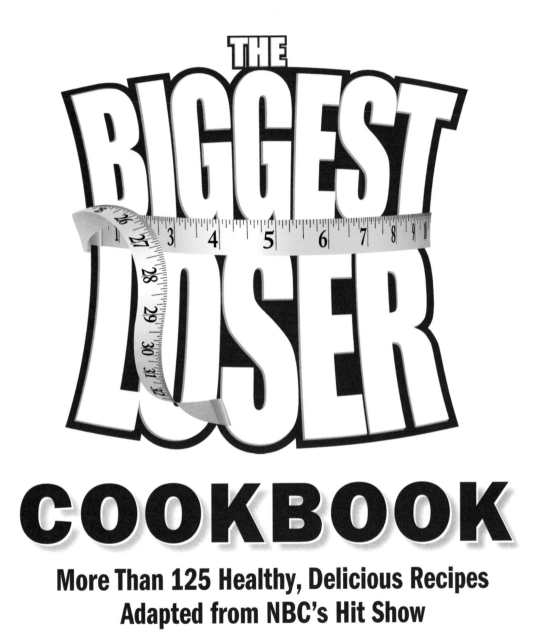

THE BIGGEST LOSER

COOKBOOK

**More Than 125 Healthy, Delicious Recipes
Adapted from NBC's Hit Show**

Chef Devin Alexander and *The Biggest Loser* Experts and Cast with Karen Kaplan
Foreword by Bob Harper and Kim Lyons

Book design by Christina Gaugler
Illustration on page 2 by Judy Newhouse
Food photographs by Mitch Mandel. All other photos by NBC Universal Photo.
Photo of Devin Alexander on page xiii by benvil photography; photo of Jeff Levine on page 20 by John Emerson; photo of Pete Thomas on pages 21 and 48 by by Elli Gurfinkel, courtesy of www.winningman.com

Library of Congress Cataloging-in-Publication Data

Alexander, Devin.
    The Biggest Loser cookbook : more than 125 healthy delicious recipes adapted from NBC's hit show / Chef Devin Alexander and The Biggest Loser experts and cast ; foreword by Bob Harper and Kim Lyons.
        p.   cm.
    Includes bibliographical references and index.
    ISBN-13 978–1–59486–575–6   paperback
    ISBN-10 1–59486–575–2   paperback
    1. Cookery.   2. Reducing diets—Recipes.   3. Biggest loser (Television program)   I. Biggest loser (Television program).   II. Title.
TX714.A433 2006
641.5'63—dc22
                                                        2006021527

Distributed to the book trade by Holtzbrinck Publishers

14 16 18 20 19 17 15   paperback

RODALE
LIVE YOUR WHOLE LIFE™

We inspire and enable people to improve their lives and the world around them
For more of our products visit **rodalestore.com** or call 800-848-4735

Contents

Foreword

Dear Reader,

You are what you eat—and I love to eat! I love to eat all kinds of food, and I *definitely* have a sweet tooth that will probably never go away. The contestants on *The Biggest Loser* also love to eat, and with our help, they learn to form a new and healthy relationship with food.

While working with the contestants on *The Biggest Loser,* one concern comes up over and over again: food. Contestants want to know what they are going to eat, and they wonder if they will ever enjoy eating healthy. When I talk to my team about food, their first thoughts are "diet, restriction, and deprivation." My contestants think I am going to take away all the food that they enjoy and force them to live on salad and broccoli. It has been a very big struggle for me to ease their fears. When new contestants come to the ranch for the first time, their whole world has been turned upside down. They are away from their family and friends and their habits—and most of all they are away from their comfort food.

In the end, they learn—as you will—that eating healthy can be quite delicious and enjoyable. Every single day, I work with food and recipes to help keep my people on track. It takes thought and structure to come up with healthy alternatives. But the good news is that Chef Devin Alexander and *The Biggest Loser* team have done all the work for you! It's all here in your two little hands.

You'll learn all the tricks and secrets we use on the ranch. You'll learn how to make these delicious and easy recipes—and you'll see that many of them take only a few minutes of prep time.

Eating healthy doesn't mean bland, tasteless food. People ask me all the time about what everyone is eating at the ranch. Many people, including the contestants at first, believe that there is some fantastic chef living with us, cooking our food, and taking care of our every need. I always laugh when I hear that. The ranch is definitely not a resort. It is a boot camp for life. The time that we spend in the gym is comparable to the time we spend in the kitchen.

I think you'll be pleasantly surprised when you use this cookbook. We found ways of cutting out the calories but leaving in all of the taste in every dish. We found ways to satisfy our sweet tooth without expanding our waists. We found ways of eating burgers and pasta without getting off our plans. Have you watched our show and wondered, "What were they eating that got them to lose so much weight?" Well, you are holding the answer. This cookbook is a great tool to get you on track. When you start eating right, it will absolutely change your life. It will make you feel better. You will have more energy. You will feel good. When you incorporate these recipes into your eating plan, you will feel the change that our contestants have felt. You will be empowered—and I will have done my job. So what are you waiting for? Get to the grocery store, get your new tools for the kitchen, and start cooking. You are really going to love it, like we all do.

Bob Harper

Dear Reader,

There are no fad diets. There are no magic pills. There are no simple answers. Those are the facts. Changing your body and your life is hard work—I'm not going to lie. But it's *so* worth it. Being healthy and fit begins with you: You making the commitment right now to change your lifestyle. I can't promise it will be easy, and I can't promise you'll always have good days, but I can promise that making the commitment will change your life forever.

Your very first life change should be your nutrition. I prefer to think of food as fuel, and since your body is a complex and demanding machine, you have to give it the best fuel possible. The sooner you start putting high-quality food into your body, the sooner you'll see amazing results, not only in your physical shape, but also in your moods and mental well-being.

Yes, it's hard. Food can be tempting. In the beginning, you'll have to be extra diligent and determined to succeed, since this is when you'll feel the most vulnerable. But trust me, you can do it. I have seen the incredible people on the show do it, and you can, too. By learning what they learn and doing what they do, you too can make significant changes in your body and person that will make jaws drop—and more important make you feel better and become healthier.

The most essential thing our contestants learn is that all meals should contain natural, whole, and unprocessed foods. If you learn nothing else, recall this phrase every time you grocery shop, dine out, or prepare a meal for your family: If God didn't make it, don't eat it! This includes all foods with more than 40 ingredients, Day-Glo coloring, or a shelf life of more than a year. That is not food. It's chemistry. So clean out your cabinets now and start over.

All the recipes contained here offer viable, tasteful, and healthy meal options that will fuel your body and your mind. But this is only the beginning. Be creative with your food. Experiment and find ways to transform your favorite old recipes into healthy new ones. Cooking with my team is one of the most rewarding parts of my job, especially since my team is continually surprised that they actually enjoy the food!

But of course we're human. Everyone will have days when the extra-cheese pizza *jumps* out of the box and lands in your mouth, or that fast-food burger sends out its tractor beam to haul you in! It happens. But remember your goal and commitment to your new lifestyle and jump right back on track.

So take this book, read it, and use it until it's in shreds! And every time you open it, renew your commitment to yourself: Imagine yourself happier, leaner, more confident, and healthier so that you stick to your plan no matter what! Now, go eat some veggies!

Yours in health,

Kim Lyons

Introduction

I f *The Biggest Loser* existed when I was in high school, I would have made every attempt known to mankind to become a contestant on the show. I was a person who always believed in herself. Indeed, some part of me secretly believed that I could achieve anything—anything, that was, except losing weight. By the time I was 15 years old, I stopped weighing myself because I just couldn't bear to see the scale creep over 175 pounds. I tried diet after diet and couldn't stick with any of them; it beat me up and made me cranky. I didn't understand why I couldn't eat what I wanted. And I had no desire to work out.

Never did I think that cooking would be the answer to my weight-loss woes. But it was. My grandmother had taught me to cook when I was very young. I always enjoyed it (probably too much), but never in a million years did I plan on being a chef. I simply started "playing in the kitchen," trying to recreate some of the dishes that I wasn't supposed to be eating on my plethora of diet plans. And it worked. I was able to make great, healthy food that made me feel that I wasn't being deprived. And although I was around food all day, I lost 55 pounds.

Not much time went by before surprised friends, colleagues, and even my own mother noticed that I was eating more and getting smaller. They were a bit worried about me until I started showing off by delivering healthy treats that were so good no one believed they were low-fat. It wasn't long before a few actresses got wind of what I was doing and tried to hire me. I ventured off to cooking school, planning to take a job as a celebrity private chef. But before I finished school, I fell into owning a catering business specializing in scrumptious cuisine for a healthy lifestyle. Word got out in Hollywood that I was throwing parties with hip, healthy food (that no one thought was healthy) and teaching celebrities how to keep eating their favorite foods without gaining weight. Soon, I started being asked to write for numerous magazines, from *Prevention* to *Men's Health.* That led to calls from producers asking me to share my secrets on TV shows such as *Good Morning America* and Discovery Health's *National Body Challenge.* And by that point, I'd signed a deal to write my first cookbook, *Fast Food Fix,* which provides recipes for healthier versions of America's fast food favorites.

Now, I feel like the luckiest girl in the world to be sharing my recipes with *The Biggest Loser* cast and fans. I started watching the show with the first episode. From the privacy of my own living room, I hoped the contestants were not feeling as deprived as I had when I started my weight-loss journey, and I wanted to help. Now I can. In this book, you will find recipes created by me, along with recipes that the cast created to help them with their exciting weight-loss transformations. My wish is that when you bite into my Boston-Cream Peanut-Butter Breakfast Banana Split, BBQ Pork Sandwich, Individual Sausage-Rigatoni Bake, or any of the other dishes, you will realize that healthy food doesn't need to be tofu-this or rabbit-food-that; it can actually taste great, which will make your journey to optimum health much easier.

Chef Devin Alexander

Notes for the Chef from the Chef

Though this book requires no special equipment to make any of the dishes, I would recommend that you consider purchasing the following items.

Olive oil sprayer. There's a big difference between olive oil spray and olive oil cooking spray. The first is a sprayer that you fill with your favorite olive oil. The latter is a pre-filled, often aerosol spray that contains propellants and other ingredients. Using an olive oil sprayer gives you the option to lightly mist extra-virgin olive oil directly onto my food to improve the texture and flavor.

Kitchen scale. Though I've tried to provide cup measurements for all ingredient amounts, I highly recommend that you invest in a kitchen scale if you truly want to live a healthy lifestyle. Often, when people are struggling with weight loss, the culprit is misjudged portion sizes.

Deli meat slicer. Most deli meats are absolutely packed with sodium (up to 900 milligrams per 4-ounce serving). And the "lower-sodium" varieties aren't much better. If you're a big fan of deli sandwiches, you may want to consider investing in a meat slicer. Over time, you will save money by cooking turkey breasts and lean roasts instead of purchasing deli meats. Plus, you'll dramatically reduce your sodium intake.

WHEN CREATING RECIPES, I'm very precise about every ingredient. Below are explanations of a few of the choices I make that might not otherwise be clear; they will help you throughout this book and in your everyday healthier cooking.

Low-carb vs. low-fat tortillas. Though low-carb tortillas have more fiber and fewer carbs, they also tend to have much more sodium. If you're concerned about your sodium intake, be sure to check the labels. Also, low-fat varieties tend to have more whole grains and natural ingredients. If you're cooking the tortillas or making pizza crusts, it's essential that you opt for low-fat since low-carb tortillas don't crisp.

Fresh herbs. Fresh herbs take time to chop, but they add loads of flavor without adding many calories. Fresh basil in a salad or fresh tarragon in an omelet can transform a boring meal into a gourmet feast—with no harm to your hips or your heart.

Fresh juices and garlic. Though it's a bit more work to use fresh juices and fresh garlic, I can't even describe how much better they taste, compared to the bottled counterparts. For me, it's the difference between truly enjoying a dish and "stomaching it."

Sodium and soups. Even though the Biggest Loser diet stresses a low-sodium intake, you'll notice that the soups in this book have higher amounts of sodium. Soups made with clear broths are vastly improved when using broth with lower sodium, as opposed to no-sodium broths. So when eating soup from this book (and many others), just be careful that your day hasn't been otherwise filled with sodium.

Ground meats. If you have trouble finding extra-lean ground turkey, chicken, pork, veal, or even beef, don't despair. The butcher at most major grocery stores will grind meats for no charge. Not only will you know it's fresh, you may even save money over buying it pre-ground. One more thing to note: If you substitute ground turkey in dishes that traditionally call for beef, you may notice that the turkey has less moisture. Ground chicken also works well as a substitute.

Cooking meats. Whether you're pan-"frying" a chicken breast, cooking beef for a fajita, or grilling a burger, it's very important to heat your pan so that it sizzles when water touches it *before* adding the meat. You also should use a pan that allows you to spread the food in a single layer. These steps ensure that you'll get a wonderful browned coating that tastes restaurant-perfect!

Low-fat vs. fat-free mayonnaise. Though the Biggest Loser diet recommends fat-free mayonnaise over low-fat, I've used low-fat throughout the book since I'm willing to trade a few grams of fat and extra calories for better taste. If you like the taste of fat-free mayonnaise, or if you're really working to maximize your weight loss, just substitute fat-free mayonnaise.

Low-fat vs. fat-free cheese. Again, I've chosen low-fat cheese over fat-free. As with mayo, it's your choice. One important note: When using low-fat or fat-free cheese, always shred it finely. You will need less to get some in every bite, and it will melt more like its full-fat counterpart.

Brown rice. I love short-grain brown rice. Though short-grain is less common, if you've only tried long grain, it might be worth a visit to your local health food store. Short-grain has a nuttier flavor and a firmer texture that I prefer.

The Biggest Loser Diet

If you're reading this book, chances are that you're looking to change your diet. Perhaps you've tried every wacky diet on the planet—the grapefruit diet, the cabbage soup diet, the brown rice diet—only to come to the realization that while most of them work in the short term, none of these diets work for the long haul. That's because wacky, extreme diets cannot be maintained—they're either unhealthy, too limiting, too boring, too depressing, or all of the above.

So if you're ready for a plan that works, you're ready for the Biggest Loser diet. It's sensible, healthy, and flexible and can be maintained for the rest of your life. It's a diet that at a certain point won't feel like a diet anymore—a diet that becomes so integrated into your life and your being that it becomes your lifestyle.

Here's what you need to know about the Biggest Loser diet: It's calorie-controlled, carbohydrate-modified, fat-reduced, and high in lean protein (which controls hunger). Let's get specific. You'll get to eat three meals and two snacks each day, so you will never be hungry or feel deprived. You can choose from an amazing, colorful variety of foods, as long as most of

THE 4-3-2-1 BIGGEST LOSER PYRAMID

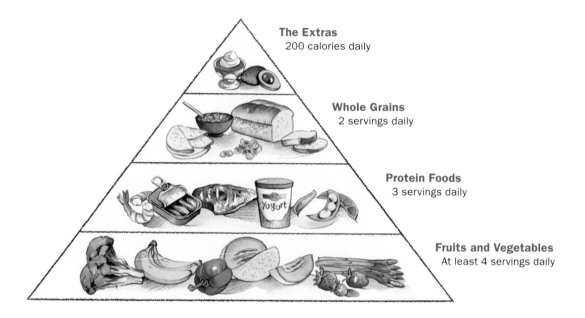

The Extras
200 calories daily

Whole Grains
2 servings daily

Protein Foods
3 servings daily

Fruits and Vegetables
At least 4 servings daily

those foods are natural and not processed. Natural foods contribute greatly to weight loss, as they are generally lower in calories, have more fiber, and are more satisfying than processed foods.

Calories Really Do Count

A calorie is the measurement of how much energy a food gives your body after you eat it. You need calories to live, and if they're the right kind of calories, you live better. But if you take in more calories than you burn through daily activity and exercise, you'll gain weight—regardless of whether those calories come from "good" natural foods or "bad" processed meals. It's that simple. The formula for losing weight is even simpler: Eat less, exercise more. But how do you know how many calories you need?

Here's the easy-to-work equation we've put together to help you: If you weigh between 150 and 300 pounds, multiply your present weight by 7. That number is your caloric goal for each day on the Biggest Loser diet. If you weigh more than 300 pounds, use 300 pounds as your starting "weight" for this formula. Likewise, if you weigh less than 150 pounds, use 150 as your starting "weight."

What Should You Eat?

In order to give the Biggest Losers an easy template to build their daily menus, we designed the 4-3-2-1 Biggest Loser Pyramid. The bottom, or widest tier, represents the fruits and vegetables in your diet. You should eat at least 4 servings daily. The next tier up represents protein foods, of which you should have 3 servings daily. The next tier is for whole grains, of which you should have 2 servings daily; and the top tier is extras, of which you can have 200 calories daily. A serving equals 8 ounces (or 1 cup), which comes out to be about the size of your hand.

Fabulous Fruits and Vegetables

On the Biggest Loser diet, fruits and vegetables are your best friends. Because these wonder foods supply the most nutrients for the fewest calories, you get to eat more of them than anything else. At least half of your 4 daily servings should be from vegetables; the other half from fruits. You may eat more than 4 daily servings if you wish, as long as you don't consume more fruit servings than vegetable servings. Almost the entire produce world is open for you to explore, but keep the following in mind:

- It's thumbs down to the white potato. Though nutritious (it's filled with potassium), it sends your blood sugar soaring, which can increase cravings for more food.
- Don't eat more than a few servings a week of starchy vegetables such as pumpkin, winter squash, sweet potatoes, and yams. While these foods offer healthy vitamins and phytonutrients, they are high in calories and carbohydrates.
- Stay away from dried fruits. They are not as filling as raw fruits, are overly concentrated in calories and fruit sugar, and are often treated with additives.
- Choose whole fruits over fruit juices. Whole fruits offer more fiber and are more filling than juices.

Powerful Protein Foods

No matter how many calories you consume each day, you must eat three 8-ounce portions of protein foods. Protein sources include animal (meat, seafood, poultry), vegetable (beans, legumes, soy), and low-fat dairy (milk, yogurt, cottage cheese). You can divide your protein however you'd like throughout the day; just make sure you eat some at each meal and that you reach your total of 24 ounces each day.

- Select a variety of proteins to consume through-out the day. That way you'll cover the nutritional spectrum and won't get bored.
- Limit red meat servings to twice a week as this protein source tends to be higher in unhealthy saturated fat.
- Avoid processed meats as they are usually high in fat and sodium nitrites.

Wonderful Whole Grains

On the Biggest Loser diet, you'll be eating two 1-cup servings of whole-grain foods each day. A whole grain is one that has undergone very little processing so that it retains its nutrients. Examples include barley, brown rice, bulgur, corn grits, cous-cous, cream of rice, cream of wheat, millet, oat bran, quinoa, rolled oats, whole-wheat cereal, whole-wheat pasta, and wild rice. Try to avoid processed or refined carbohydrates, including most ready-to-eat breakfast cereals which can be loaded with sugar. When choosing bread, look for "whole wheat" in the ingredient list. One bread serving is equal to 2 slices of whole-wheat bread (preferably "light"), 1 whole-wheat bun or roll, 1 whole-wheat flour tortilla, or 2 light Wasa crispbreads.

Extraordinary Extras

According to the Biggest Loser 4-3-2-1 Pyramid, you will be eating no more than 200 calories of extras each day. Now, 200 calories sounds like a lot, but it's not as much food as you would think—so don't blow it on appetite-stimulating foods like white bread, white pasta, white potatoes, pastries, candy, and fried snacks.

Instead, use your calorie budget wisely and spend it on healthy choices that will make your meals taste great. Extras can include oils such as olive, canola, flaxseed, and walnut; condiments such as mustard, horseradish, salsa, Tabasco, low-calorie ketchup, and low-calorie barbecue sauce; and splurges such as avocado, nuts and seeds, olives, and unsweetened pickles.

Reduced-fat, sugar-free, fat-free, and low-carb products, as tempting as they might be, should be eaten sparingly—as should artificial sweeteners—because you're aiming for meals that are as natural and nutritious as possible. Try using calorie-free extras like garlic, herbs, spices, and vinegar to perk up your meals.

What Should You Drink?

The best and easiest beverage choice is water. You should drink 6 to 8 cups each day. If you find plain old water boring, add herb sprigs, slices of cucumber, or citrus fruits.

Other beverages you can enjoy in moderation include no-calorie flavored water, coffee, tea (caffeinated or decaffeinated), and herbal teas (hot or iced). If you're one of those dieters who chugs diet sodas, it's time to go cold turkey—well, almost: You should cut back to one or two a day. Non-diet soda is off limits on the Biggest Loser diet; a 20-ounce bottle of regular soda can contain 17 teaspoons of sugar and 250 empty calories!

Alcohol, while limited, is not forbidden. You may choose to spend your daily 200 extra calories on a glass of wine, beer, or spirits. Wine, especially red, is the preferred alcohol choice as it has been proven to be heart-healthy and full of antioxidants. There are a few things to keep in mind about alcohol: It supplies calories but few nutrients; it may interfere with your body's ability to burn fat; and because it lowers inhibitions and stimulates appetite, it may cause you to engage in some unwise food choices.

What Do You Do If You Hit a Plateau?

As you lose weight, your calorie requirements will drop. For every 1 pound of weight you lose,
you decrease the number of calories you expend each day by about 10. So if you want to continue losing weight, you have to eat fewer calories, exercise more, or both. When the time comes for you to cut calories to continue dropping pounds—and that time will come—you have a number of options. We suggest that you cut calories from your extras, replace whole-grain servings with vegetables, choose lower-calorie protein foods, or replace fruit servings with vegetable servings.

And When You Feel Like Giving Up?

If you eat something you shouldn't, if you indulge on a special occasion, if you give yourself a break while on vacation, it's normal. Don't beat yourself up, and whatever you do, don't give up. Get back on track as soon as you can.

2

The Biggest Loser Exercise Plan

You can lose weight by dieting alone, but you can lose more weight faster—and get fit and healthier in the process—by adding exercise to the picture. Remember when we explained the Biggest Loser diet formula of "eat less, exercise more"? It's really that simple. Now make it your mantra.

But let's be realistic. If dieting is hard, exercising can be even harder. For many of you, it's a matter of time, or lack thereof. Your day is already jam-packed: You rise and shine, maybe you get the kids off to school, you go to work, you come home, you make dinner, you help the kids with homework, you watch TV, and you go to bed. Exactly when are you supposed to fit in an hour of exercise? The answer is, you're just going to have to make it happen—no one else can do it for you—because not exercising is not an option.

Just like you have to give up certain foods to lose weight, you're going to have to give up certain things—some TV time or your lunch hour—to get fit. But trust us, the tradeoff is worth it. After a while, it won't feel like a tradeoff anymore, because as soon as exercise becomes a part of your life, you won't be able to live without it. In fact, you won't be able to believe you ever lived without it.

As If Losing Weight and Looking Good Weren't Enough . . .

Here are 10 other reasons to get you exercising and keep you exercising:

1. You'll live longer, on average, than people who don't exercise.
2. You'll have a lower risk of getting high blood pressure or heart disease, or of having a stroke.
3. You'll have a lower risk of getting colon cancer.
4. You'll have a lower risk of getting type 2 diabetes. If you already have it, you'll lower your blood sugar levels.
5. You'll help reduce the joint swelling and pain of arthritis, and improve your mobility.
6. You'll help counter bone loss (osteoporosis).
7. You'll be functionally fit. In other words, it will be easier for you to perform necessary daily activities such as carrying groceries or lifting kids.
8. You'll have a smaller chance of getting depressed. If you're already depressed, you'll improve your chances of feeling better.
9. You'll save money on doctor visits.
10. You'll have fun! And we all need more fun in our lives.

Here's the Plan

Now you need to get started. But before you do, there are a few things to consider that might ease your fears. Remember, you are not a *Biggest Loser* cast member, so you don't have to exercise as rigorously as they do! We know that's not possible. The plan we provide here will work with your busy lifestyle. You'll be participating in both cardiovascular activity and circut training, which includes weight lifting, strength training, and stretching.

If you sign on to the safe, healthy Biggest Loser diet and exercise plan, we promise that you will get in shape in less time than you thought possible. You need to devote at least 12 weeks to the plan for maximum results, but how long you stay on the plan will vary with your goals. And, clearly, we hope that a healthy diet and daily exercise will become part of your life forever.

Butt-Busting Cardio

The best way to burn calories and fat is with cardiovascular activity. That means you've got to shake your booty—you've got to move! There are

Make sure that you check with your doctor before you start this or any exercise program.

two ways to do just that and you're going to do them both in the Biggest Loser cardio workout. The Biggest Loser exercise plan starts with steady-state cardio. *Steady-state cardio* means that you'll get your heart rate in its fat-burning zone and keep it there for a specified amount of time at a set pace. Options include walking, jogging, running, swimming, biking, dancing, working out to a DVD, and using a cardio machine like a treadmill, stair climber, stationary bicycle, or elliptical machine.

After you've gained a fitness base, you'll start to change it up with interval training. That means you'll alternate periods of high-intensity and low-intensity cardio activity. This method helps you

monitor to monitor your heart rate in the fat-burning zone.

The Biggest Loser circuit training workout will look familiar to you, as it includes push-ups, squats, shoulder presses, bicep curls, lunges, chair dips, dumbbell rows, and abdominal crunches. Begin all circuit routines with 5 minutes of walking, marching, or jogging in place, and be sure to stretch and cool down.

We recommend performing circuit training three times each week, resting at least a day between workouts.

burn more calories and fat, improves your cardiovascular fitness, and increases your speed.

Body-Sculpting Circuit Training

A circuit workout is a series of exercises (usually strength training) performed one right after another with only 5 to 8 seconds of rest in between. In circuit training, you'll alternate muscle groups, starting with one, then progressing to another. This approach creates body-firming muscle and increases aerobic capacity, all while reducing body fat. Since you'll perform in time intervals, you'll need a clock or a watch with a second hand to time yourself. You can also wear a heart rate

Do More, Lose More, Look Better

If you have extra time, consider complementing your cardio and circuit workouts with other forms of exercise. If you play tennis, racquetball, volleyball, basketball, or if you like to dance, you'll complement your conventional cardio by engaging in intense bursts of muscle activity. Yoga and Pilates also will complement your circuit by concentrating on building inner strength, core strength, and flexibility, and by teaching you proper breathing. Remember, the more you do, the more you lose! By burning 250 to 500 calories a day through exercise, you could lose up to a whole pound a week. So get to it!

For a complete guide to the Biggest Loser cardio and circuit training programs check out *The Biggest Loser: The Weight-Loss Program to Transform Your Body, Health, and Life* or *The Biggest Loser Workout, Volume 1,* on DVD, or go to the Biggest Loser Club Web site at www.biggestloserclub.com.

3

Meet the Biggest Losers

In this chapter, you'll meet the men and women who have made their weight-loss dreams come true—inspiring their friends, families, and viewers everywhere. Faced with extra pounds, health problems, and confidence issues, these people, with the help of *The Biggest Loser* team of experts, underwent dramatic weight-loss transformations.

The Trainers

Bob Harper

For more than 10 years Bob has been known as a "trainer to the stars" and has counted Gwyneth Paltrow, Ben Stiller, Ellen DeGeneres, and Guy Ritchie among his stellar clients. He is also considered a "trainer's trainer" and travels the world to educate other fitness instructors in his breakthrough technique called Function Training Method. Bob and his personal training company, based in Los Angeles, have been featured in many publications, including *Vanity Fair*, *US Weekly*, *Self*, and *Allure*. Bob encourages his cast members with his unique talent, fierce determination, and mind-body focus.

Kim Lyons

Kim has a degree in Human Development and Nutrition from Colorado State University and has been certified by the National Academy of Sports Medicine. She has written on health and exercise for *Oxygen, Muscle and Fitness*, and *Self* magazines. In addition, she is one of the fitness industry's most widely photographed models, having appeared on more than 30 covers and in many more articles. And if that weren't enough, Kim is a highly successful international fitness competitor. Not only does she have her IFBB pro card, but she was named Ms. Galaxy Fitness in 2000.

Season One

Ryan Benson

Ryan had a secret: He was a closet eater. But even though Ryan didn't tell anyone he was scarfing junk food, the 330 pounds he weighed were impossible to ignore. Once he came clean about his secret eating, he attacked his problem with a vengeance. He lost more than 100 pounds and was crowned season one's Biggest Loser. Now he's happy, healthy, a better husband, and ready for the biggest challenge of his life: having kids. Not only that, he's surfing again. Ryan is proud of his new life, which includes sticking to his new diet and exercise regimen and teaching elementary school kids about leading healthy lifestyles.

Gary Deckman

When Gary gave up smoking more than 20 years ago, the pounds crept on, but they never crept off. Eventually, Gary's eat-anything diet and lack of exercise took their toll: He had a host of weight-related medical conditions that were threatening his health. But worst of all, he couldn't keep up with his wife and kids. Fed up and frightened, he knew he had to change. Now, Gary is thin and fit and he's determined to stay that way. He eats right and runs three to five miles a day. His wife thinks he's a hunk and his kids love the new version of their dad. Gary now knows he can do anything if he puts his mind to it—even run marathons.

Kelly Minner

There were many reasons Kelly wanted to lose weight, but this teacher was especially inspired by her students. She wanted to show them that with hard work and determination, anything is possible. The look of her new slim body and the feeling of living healthily have inspired her to stay on track. She is no longer scared to see herself in the mirror, she has replaced her manic energy with a serene demeanor, and she's also learned how to reward herself without food. Kelly's dream—"inspiring her students to live healthy and believe in themselves and their potential"—is continually coming true. She spreads her inspiring weight-loss message through speaking events and through her Web site, www. kellyminner.com.

Lisa Andreone

When Lisa arrived on the Biggest Loser ranch, she weighed 236 pounds and was not happy about it. She dreamed of being able to wear a bikini, but she was even more motivated by fear: fear of dying young. Lisa knew that losing weight wasn't an option, it was essential. And lose it she did. She's now 86 pounds lighter, wears a size 8, and is focused on exercising and eating right. In turn, she has transformed from a person who described herself as "crabby, whiny, and humongous" to someone who loves to laugh and enjoys her new, healthy life.

Andrea "Drea" Baptiste

Drea was in control of every aspect of her life—other than her weight. As a former athlete and personal trainer, she couldn't believe it when she weighed in at 215 pounds. With her determination and fortitude, she lost 51 pounds and went from a size 16 to a size 6. Her days of unhealthy eating nd once-in-a-blue-moon workouts are long gone. For Drea, one of the most rewarding parts of her life has been her weight loss. She's now empowered and excited to get dressed in something hot like her little black dress. She says that losing weight was an experience in reinvention that has helped her redefine her life.

Lizzeth Davalos

When Lizzeth was growing up she always heard, "You have such a pretty face." Now, we're guessing that people tell her that she's pretty—period. That's because she took 32 pounds off her 5-foot, 1-inch frame by adopting a healthy lifestyle and turning her back on the vicious cycle of overeating and then feeling guilty. While Lizzeth was losing weight, she gained a few very important things: a sense of self-worth and the knowledge that she wasn't a quitter. Now she's helping her family get in better shape by reminding them that if at first they don't succeed, try, try again.

Dana DeSilvio

This bubbly blonde from Nashville had many reasons to lose weight: She was tired of being unhealthy, and she wanted heads to turn when she walked by. And those heads are turning now that she's slimmed down from 175 to 145 pounds and is getting a totally ripped body. Her no-nonsense approach to staying in shape includes drinking lots of water, avoiding soda, watching her sugar intake, and working out two or three times a week.

Dave Fioravanti

Hard-partying Dave ate, drank, and smoked with abandon. One day he looked in the mirror and didn't like who he saw. He also didn't like how he felt, so he knew he had to change. For Dave, going to the ranch meant giving up all of his vices—cold turkey. Though it wasn't easy at first, Dave's determination earned him the $100,000 consolation prize for losing more weight than the other eight eliminated contestants on the reunion show. And he continues on the straight and narrow, still living large but living clean. He loves being an inspiration to others, but even more, he loves being an inspiration to himself.

Matt Kamont

When Matt was a kid, he wanted to change his name because he was so tired of being teased and called "fat Matt." After appearing on *The Biggest Loser,* Matt doesn't need to worry about changing his name. He lost 70 pounds and is working on losing more. Matt is still an emotional person, but no longer an emotional eater, thanks in part to keeping a food journal. His past bingeing behaviors are long gone, and portion control is the name of his new game. Matt has been asked to teach a fitness class at the gym where he works out, and he can't wait to see the results on his clients.

Kelly MacFarland

At 223 pounds, this comedian had become so heavy that her stand-up routine had turned into one big fat joke. But all that weight on her 5-foot frame was definitely not funny. Kelly desperately wanted new material for her act, and now she has it because she has lost more than 70 pounds. She's dedicated to working out, and she's inspired her family and friends to adopt healthy lifestyles. For Kelly, it's not just about weight loss—it's also about being strong and fit. And as a road race and triathlon competitor, Kelly is certainly living that way!

Aaron Semmel

Aaron was a yo-yo dieter for most of his life, losing the same 100 pounds over and over again. An overweight teenager, he fought back in college and began competing in triathlons. As a writer, Aaron tries to live an inspired life, and he needs his body to keep up with him on his adventures. Now, Aaron is slim and trim; he likes to eat healthy and run with his dog, Triton. He's training for the world's largest triathlon in his home sweet home of Chicago. Keep on rocking, Aaron!

Maurice "Mo" Walker

At 436 pounds, Mo was afraid that his weight had made him unlucky in love and at work. But Mo was fearful of losing more than a lady or a job promotion; he was afraid of losing his life. He remembered how his overweight father had passed away from a stroke when Mo was 18, and he didn't want to carry on that legacy. Now he's on a losing streak—losing weight, that is. He's looking to get down to 235 pounds through continued devotion to diet and exercise, and he hopes to inspire the millions of other obese people out there. If he can do it, so can they.

Season Two

Matt Hoover

Matt was an Iowa high-school state champion in wrestling and then a member of four national championship teams at the University of Iowa—until an injury stopped him in his tracks. After that, he gained so much weight that competitive sports seemed like a dream. But he never lost the will to win, and that is precisely what he did. After dropping an amazing 157 pounds, he was crowned the second season's Biggest Loser. Matt has achieved his goal of "being an athlete again," and he's also found love: He and fellow cast member Suzy Preston are engaged to be married.

Seth Word

Seth wanted to see his son grow up, but he was afraid it wouldn't happen if he didn't do something about his weight. So he took the determination that he applied to his job in sales and used it to transform his body. In the process, he lost 123 pounds and became the runner-up of season two of *The Biggest Loser*. Eating right and staying fit are now integral parts of Seth's happy life with his wife and son. There's no doubt that Seth will watch his son grow up, and probably some grandkids, too!

Suzy Preston

Pretty, perky, positive Suzy spent so much time focusing on others that she often forgot to focus on herself. But that's what she had to do at the ranch in order to attain her goals of losing weight, feeling confident, and finding the man of her dreams. Little did she know that *all* of that would actually happen on *The Biggest Loser*. She lost 95 pounds, got in awesome shape, and became the season's second runner-up—and she also discovered true love with Matt Hoover, the Biggest Loser of season two. Now that's confidence!

Nick Gaza

If you're a stand-up comic, you can make jokes about your weight before other people do. That was the case with Nick, who at 346 pounds was used to making people laugh at his own expense. But that kind of weight was no laughing matter. Nick was afraid of having a heart attack and he realized he needed to do something fast. As someone who described himself as "lazy," Nick found the motivation he needed to kick-start a healthy lifestyle on *The Biggest Loser.*

Ruben Hernandez

Alternately labeled "class clown," "class flirt," and "life of the party," Ruben never had a hard time having a good time. However, he had fallen prey to unhealthy eating, and his weight wasn't what it used to be. At 278 pounds, no one was naming him "person with the best bod." After appearing on *The Biggest Loser,* Ruben was able to shape up and ship out 81 pounds. His dream of "becoming a stud again" is now a reality. He's even made a career change and is now a certified personal trainer.

Ryan Kelley

With her contagious smile and magnetic energy, Ryan is a bright light in the life of her husband, her two children, and the congregation of the church where she is music director. But there was a dark cloud hanging over Ryan's head: her size. At 225 pounds, Ryan considered her weight "out of control." Joining the cast of *The Biggest Loser* was Ryan's way of getting control of her weight, and her life. Now, after having lost 78 pounds, she feels attractive again and can fulfill her goal of wearing a top and jeans and turning her husband's head.

Jen Kersey

As a medical student, Jen wanted to be role model for her patients, but she couldn't because of her weight. With a husband, two young kids, and demanding studies, she just had no time to look after herself. At 267 pounds, her diet of convenience food from the vending machines at school was definitely taking its toll. *The Biggest Loser* gave her the jump start she needed to lose 91 pounds and transform herself from "an unhealthy couch potato into an athletic supermom." Jen used to be afraid of running, but now she can easily run six miles a day. Currently at 108 pounds, she's training to be a bodybuilder.

Jeff Levine

As a husband, father of four girls, family physician, associate professor, and director of women's health programs, Jeff never had time for himself. That meant no time to exercise and no time to eat right. That also meant a weight of 370 pounds. Jeff had lost his credibility with his patients, his self-esteem and self-respect were suffering, and he had become physically disabled. On *The Biggest Loser*, he learned that that he could make himself a priority and still be a compassionate human being. By doing so, he lost 153 pounds and became an inspiration to his family, friends, patients, colleagues, and millions of Dr. Jeff fans.

Suzanne Mendonca

As a police officer, Suzanne faced extraordinary challenges every day of her career. But one challenge she couldn't conquer was her weight. At 229 pounds, she faithfully started a diet every Monday, only to give up by midweek. Not good for an engaged woman who wanted to "be a hot bride and wear my dream wedding dress." *The Biggest Loser* turned her life around, putting her on the path to a healthy lifestyle and to a weight loss of 87 pounds.

Shannon Mullen

There are many different reasons to lose weight. Shannon, a single mom, had more than a few of her own. Her goals included eating to live and not living to eat, looking at a picture of herself and not feeling embarrassed, turning up the sexy volume, and wearing a bikini. After losing an amazing 108 pounds, we can congratulate Shannon on her accomplished mission. With the support of her sister, who has also changed her lifestyle, Shannon works to maintain her fabulous new figure.

Kathryn Murphy

Kathryn was confident about everything in her life except her weight. As a smart, self-sufficient, successful lawyer, her weight was the only case she couldn't win. She devoted so much time and energy to her work that she forgot to save some for herself. At the Biggest Loser ranch, Kathryn was able to focus on one thing and one thing only: Kathryn. Through diet and exercise she dropped pounds and reached for her goal of having "a powerful body to match my powerful mind."

Andrea Overstreet

Unlike many of the other contestants, Andrea did not always have a weight problem—in fact, she was athletic and fit most of her life. But after having kids and giving up sports, she piled on the pounds and struggled with taking them back off. Not surprisingly, Andrea wanted to regain the strong, beautiful body she once had. *The Biggest Loser* kicked her into action, and once she got moving there was no stopping her. Andrea always had a vision of herself as a healthy mom; her husband and kids say "Now that's a reality."

Pete Thomas

Pete Thomas walked away from the finale of *The Biggest Loser* a winner— and a loser. He won $100,000 for losing the highest percentage of weight among the contestants who had been voted off the show. He lost 185 pounds in nine months— and with it an unhealthy lifestyle. Armed with knowledge of better nutrition and exercise, the new Pete and his wife, Pam, run together each day, and Pete still keeps up the resistance training he learned on the ranch. Now, Pete shares his message of "modification, not starvation" with others through his Web site, www.winningman.com, and through motivational speaking to businesses, churches, and community groups.

Mark Yesitis

This San Francisco police officer, who works as a field training officer, was sick of fat jokes and doughnut shop wise- cracks. He also wanted to fit into his bullet- proof vest. But at 358 pounds, the jests were likely to keep on coming. Yet Mark figured that if he could fight crime and beat testicular cancer, he could probably lose weight. And that is exactly what this married father of two did—he lost an amazing 165 pounds. Bad guys beware: Mark is back, and he's wearing his bulletproof vest.

Season Three

Erik Chopin

Eric was an athlete growing up, but after he stopped running twice a day, he started packing on the pounds. It probably doesn't help that he works day and night at the New York deli he owns in order to provide for his wife and daughters. Though Eric's weight of 407 pounds greatly limits what he can do with his family, he is still light on his feet and often breaks out into dance moves. Eric would love to reclaim the mobility he had as an athlete and is looking to *The Biggest Loser* to help him do so.

Ken Coleman

Talk about being larger than life—that's Ken, both literally and figuratively. This paintball shop owner is 6 feet 4 inches, weighs 370 pounds, and has massive hair, a huge personality, and a contagious laugh. His five years in the military, including a stint in the Gulf War, taught Ken not to take things too seriously. But one thing he is serious about is being a role model for his wife and two teenagers. In order to do that, he knows he needs to lose weight and get healthy. He'll laugh all the way to the scale.

Jennifer Eisenbarth

This gorgeous stay-at-home mom was Miss Plus USA 1997 and a plus-size model. But at 5 feet 4 inches and 245 pounds, she's facing a cruel reality: She is too big to be a plus-size model. Talk about a wake-up call! Jennifer also wants her kids to grow up healthy, and she worries that she's setting a bad example for them. So it's out with the pizza with extra cheese that she loves, and in with a reasonable diet and exercise.

Heather Hansen

Heather is one devoted mom, wife, and friend! She takes everything she does to the next level. Always honest, Heather is sure to let you know what she is thinking or feeling. When she was younger, weight was not an issue, as she was very athletic and active. A devoted wife and recent mother, she gained the majority of the weight in the last three years. Heather came to the show ready to make a lifelong change. All heart, yet full of drive, Heather is one to watch!

friend with the good personality." And she's sick of it. She wants to get back to her former trim self and fit in with her hot friends. Though she thought it would take just a couple of weeks on the treadmill to get back into shape, Kai is learning that it's harder than it looks. But on the Biggest Loser ranch, Kai is ready to get to work in order to show off her belly button piercing again.

Tiffany Hernandez

It's hard being a single mom raising two young kids while pursing a degree in psychology. No wonder Tiffany looks to doughnut holes and cheeseburgers to take the edge off the stress of housework and homework. But Tiffany knows that food is not the answer and that at 5 feet 8 inches and 255 pounds she doesn't feel confident. She would love to be as beautiful outside as she knows she is inside.

Amy Hildreth

Blond, beautiful, and smart, Amy is working her way up the corporate ladder. She's ready to skyrocket to the top, but at 5 feet 7 inches and 260 pounds, she wants to get control of her weight once and for all. Amy has struggled with her weight since she was a child, but she's ready to put her foot down. With her fiery personality and confidence, there's no doubt she will be able to jettison pizza, pad thai, and soda for a healthy lifestyle that will enable her to realize her dreams.

Kai Hibbard

This law student is single and loves to party. But at 5 feet 5 inches and 262 pounds she's "the fat

Bobby Moore

As the cook of his firehouse, Bobby can't get away from the carbohydrate-rich food that firemen need and love. As a result, his weight is up to 321 pounds. That's hard for a guy who used to be thin and who wants to turn as many heads as his attractive wife. Bobby wants to lose weight so that he can be an inspiration to his kids and his fellow firefighters. He can't wait to bring back his healthy lifestyle regimen to the firehouse—and he can't wait to give his wife a run for the money in the looks department.

Nelson Potter

As an overweight cop, Nelson has special challenges. He is tired of breaking the steering wheel when he tries to get in and out of the police cruiser, and he's afraid that a routine foot pursuit will end badly since he can't keep up with his partner. At 6 feet 5 inches and 404 pounds, Nelson really has his work cut out for him, but he knows that losing weight will be worth the effort. As a single father of three daughters, he wants to get into shape for himself and for his girls.

Pam Smith

She's a fast-talking, simple country girl—named Miss Congeniality in her county two years in a row—who just loves fast food. When Pam was growing up, a trip to the local fast food joint was considered a family outing, and now Pam eats fast food almost every day. No doubt that habit has contributed to the 247 pounds she carries on her 5-foot, 7-inch frame. Pam was a standout athlete in high school and played softball at the college level. She would love to reclaim her athlete's body for herself, for her husband, and for her young kids.

Brian Starkey

This devoted husband and father stays at home to take care of his twin baby girls. That doesn't leave him much time to take care of himself, but he knows that he started to let himself go years ago. Brian now stands 5 feet 11 inches and weighs 308 pounds. Somewhere behind the scraggly beard and baggy clothes is a handsome man who wants to be set free.

Melinda Suttle

Melinda and her husband are happily married and would love to start a family, but one thing is holding them back: her weight. At 5 feet 5 inches and 236 pounds, she is not as healthy as she should be to get pregnant. So she is ready to say goodbye to unhealthy eating and say hello to the rigors of the Biggest Loser ranch. She'd love to win and take her husband on the honeymoon they never had—and maybe start a family in the process.

Marty Wolff

When Marty was a high school football player, he was the best; when he was the college class clown, he was the funniest; and now, when he sits down for a meal, he eats the most—he just loves double portions. But he knows that he has to stop, especially if he wants to have kids with the wife he adores and be an inspiration to the children in his classroom. As a teacher, Marty wants to inspire his pupils by losing weight and showing them what people can accomplish if they try hard.

Mark Wylie

Wylie is the good guy that everyone likes . . . as a friend. He has never been in a relationship and attributes that to his size: 6 feet 1 inch and 307 pounds. He believes that if he lost weight he would have a better shot at love. Mark works for a nonprofit organization that connects mentally handicapped people with high school and college students, and though his career is very satisfying, he believes he could be more successful if he were lighter. He's ready to leave behind his old lifestyle to get what he wants.

Special Edition: Engaged Couples

Needless to say, all four of the engaged couples had a big reason to want to lose weight: their big day.

Lael Dandan and Nick Keeler

These two successful professionals love to live the good life. In fact, their courtship revolved around wining and dining, which caused each of them to gain weight. After purchasing their first home and starting a business together, they were determined to lose weight. Nick wanted to get back into triathlons, and Lael wanted her old looks back. After appearing on *The Biggest Loser,* they've accomplished their weight-loss goals.

Kimberly (Kimmi) Dove and Bruce Lebowsky

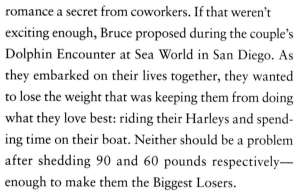

They met in an elevator at work, became close friends, and then used pseudonyms to keep their romance a secret from coworkers. If that weren't exciting enough, Bruce proposed during the couple's Dolphin Encounter at Sea World in San Diego. As they embarked on their lives together, they wanted to lose the weight that was keeping them from doing what they love best: riding their Harleys and spending time on their boat. Neither should be a problem after shedding 90 and 60 pounds respectively— enough to make them the Biggest Losers.

Sarah Eberwein and Steve Rothermel

These sweet, determined folks have stories about growing up overweight. But they didn't let the past get in the way of the future, getting married and having kids. But Sarah knew that if she wanted to fulfill her dream of being a mom, she was going to have to lose weight, and Steve knew he was going to have to lose weight to be by Sarah's side. In the end, they were successful: Steve went from 271 to 181 pounds and Sarah dropped from 297 to 220 pounds, enough to be crowned the Biggest Losers.

Rasha Spindel and Edwin Chapman

Edwin and Rasha were on an emotional and geographical roller coaster for a long time. But after Edwin was in a bad car accident, Rasha realized she was meant to be by his side. Even though getting engaged was a big accomplishment, they both had some work to do to lose weight. These two former athletes wanted to get back into competitive shape, and after losing 63 and 70 pounds respectively, Ed is back on his bike (Lance Armstrong, look out!) and Rasha is back playing softball.

Special Edition: Military Wives

With their husbands deployed to Iraq, these military wives had to deal with the stress of not knowing the well-being of their spouses. But with the help of *The Biggest Loser*, they were able to surprise their husbands with their new and improved bodies.

Marine Wives

Though these ladies had to be parents 24/7 to their little children, they were determined to take some time for themselves

to eat healthy and exercise. With this determination, it's no wonder that Amanda Carlson, Sharon Lott, Amber Gross, and Rosalinda Guadarrama lost a combined total of 125 pounds!

Navy Wives

The navy wives also struggled with finding time for themselves—and when they were stressed, food was a big comfort to them. With the help of *The Biggest Loser*, however, they learned

more healthy ways of dealing with stress. With a combined total weight loss of 151 pounds, Dari O'Brien, Jessica Lanham, Tami Bastian, and Tina Meyer were named the Biggest Losers!

Special Edition: Families

Otto Muha, Shaun Muha, and Erica Muha

As if the stress from being overweight weren't enough, the Muha family also had to deal with the fact that a member of

their family—Otto and Shaun's son and Erica's brother—was in Iraq. They wanted him to come home to a new and improved family—one that was slim and healthy. Being overweight was especially hard on 16-year-old Erica, who had her prom and graduation to look forward to. She wanted to stand up at graduation and be proud of who she had become. Proud indeed! Erica lost 52 pounds and her dad and mom lost 89 and 78 pounds respectively, enough to be crowned the Biggest Losers.

Don Samuel, Melony Samuel, and Ravee Samuel

This vivacious family has had their fair share of ups and downs, but they were determined to drop pounds and leave the weight behind. Wife Melony was diagnosed with cancer and had to have a kidney removed. Her struggle was definitely felt within the family and her recovery from cancer was an inspiration to them! Their talented daughter, Ravee, an Apollo Theater winner, believed that the only thing holding her back from success was her weight. She dreamed of joining her brother, an up-and-coming boy-band star, in Los Angeles. After appearing on *The Biggest Loser,* the family was one step closer to their dreams with a combined weight loss of 144 pounds.

Alexa Sapienza, Toni Sapienza, Daniela Drago, and Robert Iovane

This Italian family spent long hours running their restaurant in the Bronx. That meant they were around food—rich and fattening Italian food—all of the time. With a little taste here and a little taste there and no time to exercise, before they knew it, the family was overweight. Mother Toni, daughter Alexa, and cousins Daniela and Robert all knew that they had to get out of the restaurant to jump-start their weight loss, but also knew that they had to gain the skills to continue losing weight in a restaurant environment. That's exactly what they did—and also lost a grand total of 169 pounds.

Scott Senti, Tammy Senti, Emily Senti, and Kelly Wilcox

Everyone in Peoria, Illinois knew about the Maid-Rite diner owned by the Senti family. Customers were tempted by the incredible hamburgers, fries, shakes, and, especially, the apple pie. Of course, the Sentis were tempted, too, and that was a problem. Mom, Dad, and their two daughters were all overweight. It was especially hard on the youngest daughter, Emily, who was teased so much at school that she attended only once a week. Scott and Tammy desperately wanted to change the dynamic of their defeated family and they did: On *The Biggest Loser,* the family lost a combined total of 242 pounds. No wonder they were crowned the Biggest Losers.

4

Breakfasts

Remember how your mom used to say, "Breakfast is the most important meal of the day"? Well, believe it or not, your mom was right—and her words of wisdom have been validated by the most recent studies in nutrition. These studies show that skipping breakfast can be a big contributor to weight gain.

So why is breakfast so important? First of all, you need it. Most of us use up more energy during the morning hours and therefore need the long-lasting fuel provided by a well-balanced breakfast. Even better, breakfast keeps you from getting hungry later in the day. If you eat a healthy meal in the morning, you will be less tempted to overeat in the afternoon—leading to better food choices throughout the day. In addition, breakfast kick-starts your brain, your body—and best of all, your metabolism—so that you think better, live better, and burn calories more efficiently.

Try carving out time for breakfast; you might really enjoy it. A relaxed morning meal can set the tone for a cheerful, productive day. And there's no better way to start off a day on the Biggest Loser diet than with Warm Pumpkin-Pie Cream of Wheat or a Mango Strawberry Breakfast Sundae.

Maybe you don't always have time for breakfast. In that case, try the low-fat Sausage, Egg, and Cheese Breakfast Sandwich or the Energizing Bacon and Egg Breakfast Burrito. Both recipes take only moments to prepare, and they're portable as well as delicious.

BOSTON-CREAM PEANUT-BUTTER BREAKFAST BANANA SPLIT

Who doesn't want a banana split . . . any time of the day? Here's one that's not only so decadent you'll forget you're eating healthy, it's so fun, you're likely to feel like a kid again—a kid getting away with eating "junk food" for breakfast.

---

1 small ripe banana (about 6" long), peeled and halved lengthwise

1 tablespoon reduced-fat peanut butter

⅓ cup low-fat, artificially sweetened Boston cream pie–flavored yogurt

2 tablespoons crunchy high-fiber, low-sugar cereal (such as Grape-Nuts)

Place the banana halves in a small banana split dish or shallow bowl, with the cut sides facing inward. Spread the peanut butter evenly over the open banana. Spoon the yogurt in the middle. Top with the cereal. Serve immediately.

Makes 1 serving

Per serving: **294 calories, 8 g protein, 53 g carbohydrates, 7 g fat (2 g saturated), 3 mg cholesterol, 5 g fiber, 241 mg sodium**

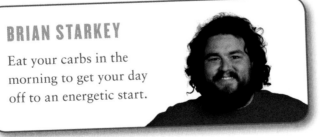

BRIAN STARKEY

Eat your carbs in the morning to get your day off to an energetic start.

MANGO STRAWBERRY BREAKFAST SUNDAE

This is one of those dishes that you may take one bite and think is a bit bizarre—but then will keep eating anyway. Without fail, the bowl will get emptied. In the summer months, it's particularly great to start the day with this cool, refreshing treat.

1 cup unsweetened frozen strawberries

½ cup chopped mango

¼ cup orange juice (preferably fresh squeezed)

4 ice cubes

½ teaspoon honey (optional)

¼ cup crunchy, high-fiber, low-sugar cereal (such as Grape-Nuts)

In a blender, combine the strawberries, mango, juice, and ice. On high speed, blend until the mixture is almost smooth with a consistency somewhere between a slush and a sorbet. Pour into a cereal bowl or tall glass. Stir in the honey, if desired. Top with the cereal. Serve immediately.

Makes 1 serving

Per serving: 238 calories, 5 g protein, 58 g carbohydrates, 1 g fat (trace saturated), 0 mg cholesterol, 7 g fiber, 182 mg sodium

TRAINER TIP: **BOB HARPER**

In the summer, go to the farmers' market; you can find so many different fruits and vegetables to choose from. Try something different that you've never ever eaten before.

CHOCOLATE-CHERRY BREAKFAST SMOOTHIE

Chocolate for breakfast? Absolutely. When I'm craving chocolate in the morning, I head straight to the blender for this quick-to-prepare favorite. Though it's made with cocoa (and thus satisfies the chocolate craving), it isn't sugary-sweet, so it won't set you up to crave sugar all day.

¾ cup frozen unsweetened sweet cherries (not thawed)

½ cup sugar-free, fat-free vanilla yogurt

¼ cup fat-free milk

1 tablespoon unsweetened cocoa powder

4 ice cubes

1 teaspoon honey (optional)

In the jar of a blender, combine the cherries, yogurt, milk, cocoa, and ice cubes. Blend on high speed or ice-crush setting for 30 to 60 seconds, or until smooth. Stir in the honey, if desired. Pour into a glass. Serve immediately.

Makes 1 (12-ounce) serving

Per serving: **160 calories, 8 g protein, 33 g carbohydrates, 1 g fat (trace saturated), 4 mg cholesterol, 4 g fiber, 97 mg sodium**

WARM PUMPKIN-PIE CREAM OF WHEAT

If you love pumpkin pie, it's likely you'll make this dish a staple during those chilly fall mornings. Though the Grape-Nuts are not needed, they add a very nice contrasting texture that really satisfies. With only 26 calories and a trace of fat per tablespoon, you can't go wrong adding them.

¼ cup canned pumpkin

2 packets (.035 ounce each) sugar substitute (such as Splenda)

¼ teaspoon ground cinnamon

Pinch of ground ginger, or to taste

Pinch of ground cloves, or to taste

Pinch of salt

1 packet (1 ounce) instant Cream of Wheat cereal

⅔ cup boiling water

1 tablespoon crunchy, high-fiber, low-sugar cereal, such as Grape-Nuts (optional)

In a microwaveable serving bowl, combine the pumpkin, sugar substitute, cinnamon, ginger, cloves, and salt. Stir to mix. Microwave on low power, checking every 15 seconds, for 30 to 45 seconds, or until warm.

In a serving bowl, stir together the Cream of Wheat and boiling water. Stir in the pumpkin mixture. Sprinkle the crunchy cereal on top, if desired.

Makes 1 serving

Per serving: **121 calories, 4 g protein, 24 g carbohydrates, trace fat (trace saturated), 0 mg cholesterol, 4 fiber, 319 mg sodium**

BETTER BLUEBERRY PANCAKES

If you're as big a fan of these pancakes as my brunching buddies and I are, rest assured that you can double, triple, and even quadruple this recipe with great success. In addition, the batter will keep in your refrigerator for up to 3 days. I personally like to mix the batter fresh and enjoy the pancakes with a friend . . . otherwise, I find myself tempted to eat more than one serving.

½ cup reduced-fat buttermilk

½ cup whole-grain oat flour

1 large egg white, lightly beaten

½ teaspoon baking soda

¼ teaspoon vanilla extract

¼ teaspoon salt

I Can't Believe It's Not Butter! spray

½ cup fresh or frozen (not thawed) blueberries

Sugar-free, low-calorie pancake syrup (optional)

100% fruit orange marmalade spread (optional)

Preheat the oven to 200°F.

In a small bowl, combine the buttermilk, flour, egg white, baking soda, vanilla, and salt. Whisk just until blended. Stir in the blueberries. Let stand for 10 minutes.

Heat a large nonstick skillet over medium heat until it is hot enough for a spritz of water to sizzle on it. With an oven mitt, briefly remove the pan from the heat to mist lightly with I Can't Believe It's Not Butter! cooking spray. Return the pan to the heat. Pour the batter in ⅛-cup dollops onto the skillet to form 3 or 4 pancakes. Cook for about 2 minutes, or until bubbles appear on the tops and the bottoms are golden brown. Flip. Cook for about 2 minutes, or until browned on the bottom. Transfer to an oven-proof plate. Cover with aluminum foil. Place in the oven to keep warm. Repeat with cooking spray and the remaining batter to make 8 pancakes total.

Place 4 pancakes on each of 2 serving plates. Serve immediately with I Can't Believe It's Not Butter! spray, syrup, and/or fruit spread, if desired.

Makes 2 (4-pancake) servings

Per serving: **140 calories, 8 g protein, 20 g carbohydrates, 3 g fat (less than 1 g saturated), 5 mg cholesterol, 3 g fiber, 687 mg sodium**

LEMON–POPPY SEED MINI-MUFFINS

If you're like me and have an undying sweet tooth, these muffins are the perfect solution. Though I tend to eat them for breakfast after I've "been good" and had an egg white omelet, they're actually perfect for any time of the day. They're tiny, yet satisfying (as opposed to "so weirdly addicting I want to eat every last one of them"). With only about 40 calories and a half-gram of fat each, how can you go wrong with one or two?

I Can't Believe It's Not Butter! spray

1 cup whole grain oat flour

¼ teaspoon baking soda

¼ teaspoon baking powder

¼ teaspoon salt

½ cup fat-free, artificially sweetened vanilla yogurt

3 large egg whites

⅓ cup honey

1 teaspoon vanilla extract

½ teaspoon lemon extract

1 tablespoon grated lemon peel

2 teaspoons poppy seeds

Preheat the oven to 350°F. Coat 20 cups of a mini-muffin tin with nonstick I Can't Believe It's Not Butter! cooking spray. In the bowl of a food processor fitted with the metal blade, process the flour for about 1 minute, or until it is the consistency of all-purpose flour and no coarse grains remain. Combine the flour, baking soda, baking powder, and salt. Sift the mixture twice.

In a medium mixing bowl, combine the yogurt, egg whites, honey, vanilla extract, and lemon extract with a sturdy whisk or spatula until well mixed. Stir in the reserved flour mixture until just combined. Stir in the lemon peel and poppy seeds. Spoon the batter into the 20 prepared muffin cups.

Bake for 9 to 11 minutes, or until a toothpick inserted in the center of one muffin comes out dry (a few crumbs are okay). Cool in the pan on a rack for 5 minutes then remove the muffins to the rack.

Makes 20 mini-muffins

Per muffin: **41 calories, 1 g protein, 8 g carbohydrates, less than 1 g fat (trace saturated), trace cholesterol, less than 1 g fiber, 64 mg sodium**

SHARON'S APPLE-CINNAMON-MUFFIN OATMEAL

Sharon Lott created this recipe when she got bored eating plain oatmeal. She says, "I feel like I am having an apple-cinnamon muffin when I eat this." She sometimes adds a few more sprays of I Can't Believe It's Not Butter! spray, but she tries to go light on it ever since we taught her that it does *have calories and fat if you use more than a few spritzes.*

I Can't Believe It's Not Butter! spray

3 Granny Smith or other baking apples, coarsely chopped

2 teaspoons ground cinnamon

1 teaspoon vanilla extract

2 cups water

Pinch of salt

1 cup old-fashioned oats

2 to 3 packets (.035 ounce each) sugar substitute (such as Splenda)

3 tablespoons chopped raw almonds or walnuts (optional)

Lightly coat a medium nonstick frying pan with I Can't Believe It's Not Butter! spray. Place it over medium heat. Add the apples, cinnamon, vanilla extract, and 5 spritzes of I Can't Believe It's Not Butter! spray. Cook, stirring occasionally, for about 20 minutes, or until the apples are soft.

Meanwhile, in a medium saucepan, bring the water and salt to a full boil. Add the oats. Reduce the heat to medium and cook, stirring occasionally, for 6 minutes, or until the water is almost absorbed. Remove from the heat and cover.

When the apples are cooked, stir the apple mixture into the oatmeal. Stir in 2 packets of sugar substitute and the nuts, if desired. Taste and add 1 more packet of sugar substitute, if desired. Spoon into 3 serving bowls. Serve immediately.

Makes 3 (generous 1⅓-cup) servings

Per serving: **218 calories, 6 g protein, 44 g carbohydrates, 3 g fat (less than 1 g saturated), 0 mg cholesterol, 7 g fiber, 74 mg sodium**

SUNRISE OATMEAL

This oatmeal is a particularly great choice for those who prefer not to use artificial sweeteners. Cooking it in orange juice adds sweetness without using refined or unnatural sweeteners. If it's at all possible, definitely used fresh-squeezed orange juice. If not, then be sure to opt for one that is "not from concentrate."

½ cup orange juice,
   preferably fresh squeezed

½ cup water

   Pinch of salt

½ cup old-fashioned oats

¼ cup blueberries

½ teaspoon orange extract

In a small saucepan, combine the juice, water, and salt over high heat. Bring the mixture to a rolling boil. Add the oats and reduce the heat to medium. Cook, stirring occasionally, for 5 to 7 minutes, or until the liquid is almost gone. Cover the pan and remove it from the heat. Set aside for 5 minutes. Stir in the blueberries and orange extract. Spoon into a serving bowl. Serve immediately.

Makes 1 serving

Per serving: 243 calories, 8 g protein, 45 g carbohydrates, 3 g fat (trace saturated), 0 mg cholesterol, 5 g fiber, 147 mg sodium

DANA DESILVIO

Post a picture of yourself at your worst on the refrigerator. So the next time you're thinking of grabbing something you shouldn't from the fridge, you'll be reminded of what you don't want to look like.

NELSON'S CHILLY MORNING GRAPE-NUTS BOWL

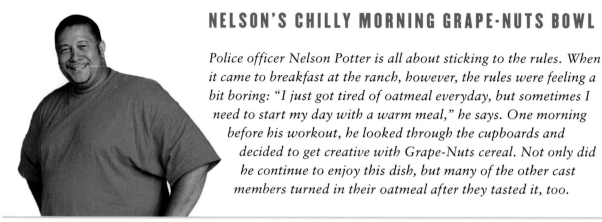

Police officer Nelson Potter is all about sticking to the rules. When it came to breakfast at the ranch, however, the rules were feeling a bit boring: "I just got tired of oatmeal everyday, but sometimes I need to start my day with a warm meal," he says. One morning before his workout, he looked through the cupboards and decided to get creative with Grape-Nuts cereal. Not only did he continue to enjoy this dish, but many of the other cast members turned in their oatmeal after they tasted it, too.

½ cup Grape-Nuts or other crunchy high-fiber, low-sugar cereal

½ cup fat-free vanilla soy milk

1 tablespoon raisins

1 to 2 packets (.035 ounce each) sugar substitute (such as Splenda)

In a microwaveable cereal bowl, combine the cereal, soy milk, and raisins. Microwave on high power for 2 to 3 minutes, or until the cereal has absorbed the milk. Stir in 1 to 2 packets sugar substitute to taste. Serve immediately.

Makes 1 serving

Per serving: 284 calories, 10 g protein, 62 g carbohydrates, 1 g fat (trace saturated), 0 mg cholesterol, 6 g fiber, 408 mg sodium

MAURICE WALKER

Stay away from the middle of the grocery store. That's where all the processed food is. Shop in the outer aisles, where you'll find fresh fruits, vegetables, meat, fish, and poultry.

OTTO'S TASTY EGG-WHITE OMELET

Otto Muha loves to start his day with this omelet. Though he suggests using much more garlic and onion, I like to keep this one a bit milder. If you're headed off to work or have a hot date, you may want to join me and follow the recipe below as is. Otto also uses fat-free American cheese. If you're trying to maximize results, you may consider that. Cabot's 75% Light Cheddar Cheese, on the other hand, adds only 30 calories and 2½ grams of fat. I personally think it's well worth the splurge.

½ cup fresh or thawed frozen broccoli, finely chopped

¼ cup chopped red onion

1 clove garlic, minced

¾ cup fresh spinach leaves

4 large egg whites

⅛ teaspoon ground black pepper

½ cup (1 ounce) finely shredded Cabot 75% Light Cheddar Cheese

Salt, to taste

3 tablespoons picante sauce (optional)

Mist a medium nonstick skillet with olive oil spray. Set over medium heat. Add the broccoli, onion, and garlic. Cook, stirring occasionally, for 4 to 6 minutes, or until the onion is almost tender. Add the spinach and cook for 1 to 2 minutes, or until wilted. Remove the vegetables to a plate. Cover and set aside to keep warm.

In a small bowl, whisk the egg whites and pepper until the egg whites bubble lightly. Coat the pan with olive oil spray. Set over medium heat. Pour the egg white mixture into the pan. Cook, lifting the edges with a spatula as they start to set and tipping the pan for uncooked egg whites to run underneath, for 2 to 3 minutes, or until almost set. Flip the omelet. Spoon the reserved vegetables over the egg-white mixture. Sprinkle the cheese evenly over the top. Cover and cook for 1 to 2 minutes, or until the cheese is melted. Fold the omelet in half. Transfer to a serving plate. Season with salt. Top with picante sauce, if desired. Serve immediately.

Makes 1 serving

Per serving: **160 calories, 24 g protein, 11 g carbohydrates, 3 g fat (1 g saturated), 6 mg cholesterol, 3 g fiber, 435 mg sodium**

MARK'S SOUTHWESTERN OMELET

Since his days on the ranch, Mark Yesitis has enjoyed creating various omelets for breakfast. This one, however, has quickly become one of his favorites. He says it not only tastes great, it's very filling even though it has only about 120 calories. It's a great choice to enjoy with one or two Lemon–Poppy Seed Mini-Muffins (page 41).

¾ cup egg substitute or 6 egg whites

2 tablespoons minced green or red bell pepper

2 tablespoons minced fresh tomato

1 tablespoon minced mushroom

1 teaspoon minced onion

3 tablespoons salsa

1 tablespoon light or fat-free sour cream

In a medium bowl, combine the egg substitute or egg whites, bell pepper, tomato, mushroom, and onion.

Mist a medium nonstick skillet with olive oil spray. Set over medium heat. Add the egg substitute mixture to the pan. Cook, lifting the edges with a spatula as they start to set and tipping the pan for uncooked egg substitute or egg whites to run underneath, for 3 to 5 minutes, or until almost set. Flip the omelet. Cook for 1 minute, or until set. Fold the omelet in half. Transfer to a serving plate. Top with salsa and sour cream. Serve immediately.

Makes 1 serving

Per serving: **122 calories, 17 g protein, 8 g carbohydrates, 2 g fat (less than 1 g saturated), 5 mg cholesterol, less than 1 g fiber, 428 mg sodium**

SETH'S FIESTA POACHED EGGS

Seth Word loves eating sweet treats for breakfast, but he knew he needed to get in some protein, too. So he created this low-cal protein dish that's easy to prepare. "I just throw a couple of egg whites in a poacher and play with my son," he says. "When they're done, it's simple to put them in a bowl with fresh, store-bought pico de gallo." When he's finished, he follows the eggs with a Pumpkin-Walnut Snack Muffin (page 210) or a couple of Better Blueberry Pancakes (page 38), which creates a perfect nutrient balance and satisfies his sweet tooth.

3 large egg whites

½ cup fresh salsa or pico de gallo, drained

Fill a shallow pan with about 2" of water. Set over high heat. Place an egg poacher insert or 3 small, ovenproof bowls (or ramekins) into the water. The water should not reach the top of the bowls. If it does, pour some out.

Dry the poacher inserts or bowls and then mist with olive oil spray. Place 1 egg white in each poacher insert or bowl. When the water boils, reduce the heat to low and cover the pan. Cook for about 7 minutes, or until the egg whites are completely set. Run a butter knife carefully around the inner edges of the poacher inserts or bowls to loosen the egg whites.

Spoon the salsa into a shallow serving bowl. Turn the poached egg whites onto the salsa. Serve immediately.

Makes 1 serving

Per serving: **79 calories, 11 g protein, 9 g carbohydrates, less than 1 g fat (0 g saturated), 0 mg cholesterol, 0 g fiber, 226 mg sodium**

PETE'S MAN-SIZE LOW-CALORIE BREAKFAST OMELET

Pete Thomas often refers to this, one of his favorite dishes, as the Garbage-Can Breakfast. He uses the recipe as a general guideline, but basically grabs all of the veggies from his refrigerator at any given time and creates a one-of-a-kind omelet.

1 uncooked Biggest Winner Breakfast Sausage patty (page 51), crumbled

½ cup chopped onion

½ cup sliced mushrooms

¼ cup chopped green bell pepper

¼ cup chopped red bell pepper

¼ cup chopped yellow bell pepper

¼ cup chopped orange bell pepper

½ cup Cheese & Chive Egg Beaters

1 wedge (¾ ounce) Laughing Cow Light Garlic & Herb cheese, chopped

Salt, to taste

Ground black pepper, to taste

Set a medium nonstick skillet over medium-high heat until it is hot enough for a spritz of water to sizzle on it. With an oven mitt, briefly remove from the heat to mist with olive oil spray. Place the sausage, onion, mushrooms, and bell peppers in the pan. Cook, stirring occasionally, for 4 to 6 minutes, or until the sausage is no longer pink and the vegetables are tender. Remove from the pan. Cover and set aside to keep warm.

Mist the pan with olive oil spray. Set over medium heat. Add the Egg Beaters. Cook, lifting the edges with a spatula as they start to set and tipping the pan for uncooked Egg Beaters to run underneath, for 2 to 3 minutes, or until almost set. With a spatula, flip the omelet. Scatter the cheese evenly over half of the egg mixture. Top with the reserved vegetables. Fold the omelet in half. Cook for about 1 minute, or until the cheese melts. Transfer to a serving plate. Season with salt and pepper. Serve immediately.

Makes 1 serving

Per serving: 213 calories, 24 g protein, 22 g carbohydrates, 4 g fat (1 g saturated), 28 mg cholesterol, 4 g fiber, 605 mg sodium

ASPARAGUS MINI-QUICHES

This is an excellent recipe to serve to company for breakfast, lunch, or even as a dinner appetizer. It does require a 3¾" cookie cutter. If you don't have one, don't worry. You can use an empty 3¾"-diameter can or simply cut 3¾" circles using a butter knife. Whatever you do, however, don't try this recipe with low-carb tortillas—they'll burn instead of crisping.

I Can't Believe It's Not Butter! spray

½ cup chopped red onion

1 large clove garlic, minced

⅓ cup fat-free milk

6 large egg whites

2 teaspoons Dijon mustard

Salt, to taste

Ground black pepper, to taste

6 whole-wheat flour, 96% fat-free tortillas (8" diameter)

1½ cups (3 ounces) finely shredded Cabot 75% Light Cheddar Cheese

4 medium asparagus spears, thinly sliced into small disks

Preheat the oven to 375°F. Coat 12 cups of a standard size, nonstick muffin tin with I Can't Believe It's Not Butter! spray. Set aside.

Mist a small nonstick skillet with cooking spray and set over medium heat. Add the onion and garlic. Cook, stirring occasionally, for about 5 minutes, or until almost tender. Remove the pan from the heat and set aside.

In a large measuring cup, combine the milk, egg whites, mustard, salt, and pepper. Whisk to mix well. Set aside.

With a 3¾" round cookie cutter, cut circles out of each tortilla. Being careful not to tear the circles, fit each into one of the 12 cups in the prepared tin. Divide the cheese, asparagus, and reserved onion mixture among the cups. Add the egg-white mixture, dividing evenly, until each cup is three-quarters filled. (If a small amount is leftover, discard it.)

Bake for 20 to 22 minutes, or until the egg-white mixture is set and the tortillas are lightly crisped around the edges. Serve immediately.

Makes 4 (3-quiche) servings

Per serving: **185 calories, 15 g protein, 24 g carbohydrates, 3 g fat (less than 1 g saturated), 5 mg cholesterol, 3 g fiber, 549 mg sodium**

BIGGEST WINNER BREAKFAST SAUSAGE

I particularly love this sausage as part of breakfast sandwiches or chopped in omelets or other egg dishes. If you're eating it on its own, a bit more salt is advised (from a flavor standpoint) to make it taste like full-fat sausage that still has a small fraction of the fat and calories. For those who don't eat pork, chicken or turkey can be substituted, but again, added salt is definitely needed.

½ pound extra-lean ground pork or pork tenderloin, ground

1 tablespoon minced red onion

1½ teaspoons minced garlic

½ teaspoon dried thyme

¼ teaspoon ground sage

¼ teaspoon cayenne

¼ teaspoon ground black pepper

⅛ teaspoon salt

In a medium mixing bowl, combine the pork, onion, garlic, thyme, sage, cayenne, black pepper, and salt. With clean hands or a fork, mix well. Divide the mixture into 4 equal parts. Shape each into a ball. On a sheet of waxed paper, flatten one ball into a 4"-diameter patty. Repeat with the remaining balls. Place any patties that won't immediately be cooked in a single layer or stacked between sheets of waxed paper in an airtight plastic container. Refrigerate for up to 3 days or freeze for up to 1 month

To cook, select a skillet that's the appropriate size to hold the patty or patties to be cooked in a single layer. Set the skillet over medium-high heat until it is hot enough for a spritz of water to sizzle on it. With an oven mitt, briefly remove the pan from the heat to mist with olive oil spray. Set the patty or patties in the pan. Cook for 1 to 2 minutes per side, or until just starting to brown and no longer pink inside. Serve immediately.

Makes 4 patties

Per patty: **72 calories, 12 g protein, 1 g carbohydrates, 2 g fat (less than 1 g saturated), 37 mg cholesterol, trace fiber, 101 mg sodium**

SAUSAGE, EGG, AND CHEESE BREAKFAST SANDWICH

This is probably one of my all-time favorite breakfast dishes. And if you keep the sausage patties on hand, you can throw this together quicker than you could even make it through the drive-thru. Though I'm generally not a fan of fat-free cheese, I don't mind it in this recipe.

1 uncooked Biggest Winner Breakfast Sausage patty (page 51)

1 large egg white

1 whole-grain English muffin

1 slice (¾ ounce) fat-free yellow American cheese

Set a 3½" round metal cookie cutter to one side in a medium nonstick skillet. Set the pan over medium-high heat until it is hot enough for a spritz of water to sizzle on it. Mist the skillet and the inner ring of the cutter with olive oil spray. Place the sausage on one side of the pan. Cook for 1 to 2 minutes per side, or until the sausage is no longer pink inside. Meanwhile, drop the egg white into the cookie cutter. Cook for 1 to 2 minutes, or until the egg white sets in the middle and the bottom starts to brown. Carefully (wearing an oven mitt) use a butter knife to loosen the egg white from the cutter. Remove the cutter and flip the egg white. Cook for 1 to 2 minutes, or until completely set. Remove from the heat.

Meanwhile toast the muffin. Set the muffin bottom, cut-side up, on a plate. Top with the sausage, the cheese, the cooked egg white, and the muffin top. Serve immediately.

Makes 1 serving

Per serving: **278 calories, 27 g protein, 34 g carbohydrates, 4 g fat (1 g saturated), 40 mg cholesterol, 2 g fiber, 707 mg sodium**

SAUSAGE BREAKFAST SCRAMBLE

Though I rarely cook food in the microwave (like most chefs), I prefer scrambled egg whites prepared in the microwave to those made in a pan. Once you've done it a few times, you can achieve perfect, fluffy "scrambled eggs" that are not watery in the least or overcooked—the way they tend to turn out when cooked in a pan without added fat. This is a delicious recipe to use for practice . . . and it's utter enjoyment with limited fat and calories.

---

4 large egg whites

1 uncooked Biggest Winner Breakfast Sausage patty (page 51), crumbled

¼ cup chopped onion

¼ cup chopped red bell pepper

¼ teaspoon seeded, chopped jalapeño chile pepper (wear plastic gloves when handling)

Salt, to taste

Ground black pepper, to taste

Hot-pepper sauce (optional)

Mist a medium microwaveable bowl with olive oil spray. Add the egg whites. Set aside.

Mist a small nonstick skillet with olive oil spray. Set over medium-high heat. Place the sausage, onion, bell pepper, and chile pepper in the pan. Cook, stirring with a wooden spoon, for 3 to 5 minutes, or until the sausage is no longer pink.

Meanwhile, microwave the egg whites on low power for 30 seconds. Continue microwaving them in 30-second intervals until they are just a bit runny on top. Stir with a fork, breaking them apart into large pieces. If they are still undercooked, cook them in 10-second intervals until set. Stir into the sausage mixture. Season with salt, black pepper, and hot-pepper sauce, if desired. Spoon onto a serving plate. Serve immediately.

Makes 1 serving

Per serving: **168 calories, 27 g protein, 8 g carbohydrates, 3 g fat (less than 1 g saturated), 37 mg cholesterol, 1 g fiber, 326 mg sodium**

BRIAN'S BREAKFAST SCRAMBLE

Brian Starkey never used to like egg whites because he thought they always turned out watery. Once he learned that scrambled egg whites work much better in the microwave, he was hooked. Brian started creating all sorts of veggie combos to keep variety in his breakfasts. He has only three words about this version: "Um, um, good!"

3 tablespoons chopped green bell pepper

3 tablespoons chopped onion

3 tablespoons seeded and chopped tomato

6 large egg whites (¾ cup)

¾ cup (1½ ounces) finely shredded Cabot 75% Light Cheddar Cheese

Salt, to taste

Ground black pepper, to taste

Place a small nonstick skillet over medium-high heat until it is hot enough for a spritz of water to sizzle on it. With an oven mitt, briefly remove the pan from the heat to mist lightly with olive oil spray. Add the green pepper and onion. Cook, stirring occasionally, for 3 to 5 minutes, or until tender. Add the tomato. Cook for about 1 minute, or until just warm. Set aside.

Meanwhile, lightly mist a medium microwaveable bowl with olive oil spray. Add the egg whites. Microwave on low power for 30 seconds. Continue microwaving in 30-second intervals until the egg whites are just a bit runny on top. Stir with a fork, breaking them apart into large pieces. If they are still undercooked, cook in 10-second intervals until set. Stir the reserved vegetable mixture and the cheese into the egg whites. Season with salt and pepper. Serve immediately.

Makes 1 serving

Per serving: 222 calories, 36 g protein, 8 g carbohydrates, 5 g fat (2 g saturated), 15 mg cholesterol, 1 g fiber, 640 mg sodium

ENERGIZING BACON AND EGG BREAKFAST BURRITO

Before I moved to LA, I'd never seen anyone eat a burrito for breakfast. But when I first started teaching healthy cooking, one of my clients said he "would die" before he gave up his breakfast burritos. I quickly jumped to the task. Not only has he been eating this one ever since, so have I (though I tend to use a low-carb, whole-wheat tortilla).

3 large egg whites

1 strip nitrate-free turkey bacon, chopped

¼ cup chopped onion

2 tablespoons seeded, chopped fresh tomato

1 whole-wheat flour, 96% fat-free tortilla (8" diameter)

¼ cup (½ ounce) finely shredded Cabot 75% Light Cheddar Cheese

2 teaspoons red taco sauce

Mist a small microwaveable bowl with olive oil spray. Add the egg whites. Set aside.

Set a small nonstick skillet over medium-high heat until it is hot enough for a spritz of water to sizzle on it. With an oven mitt, briefly remove the pan from the heat to mist with cooking spray. Set over medium-high heat and add the bacon. Cook, stirring occasionally, for about 2 minutes. Add the onion. Cook for 1 to 2 minutes, or until the bacon is crisp. Add the tomato. Cook for about 1 minute, or until just heated. Transfer the bacon mixture to a bowl. Cover to keep warm. Place the tortilla in the pan and return to medium-high heat. Cook for about 30 seconds per side, or until just warm.

Meanwhile, microwave the egg whites on low power for 30 seconds. Continue microwaving in 30-second intervals until they are just a bit runny on top. Stir them with a fork, breaking into large pieces. If they are still undercooked, cook them in 10-second intervals until just done. Stir in the reserved bacon mixture.

Place the tortilla on a serving plate. Sprinkle on the cheese leaving about 2" bare on one end, in an even strip (about 3" wide) running down the center. Top with the reserved egg white mixture and drizzle on the taco sauce. Fold the bare end of the tortilla up over the filling, and then fold the sides of the tortilla over the middle. Serve immediately.

Makes 1 serving

Per serving: **251 calories, 24 g protein, 30 g carbohydrates, 5 g fat (less than 1 g saturated), 28 mg cholesterol, 3 g fiber, 630 mg sodium**

CINNAMON-APPLE BREAKFAST POCKETS

At first glance, the ingredients in this breakfast may sound like a bit of a wacky combination. But if you like apples and yogurt, you just have to give this a try. It's a surprisingly tasty treat that can get your morning started off on the right foot—especially if you love sweets as much as I do.

---

1 whole-wheat pita
(6½" diameter) cut
in half

4 tablespoons fat-free,
artificially sweetened
vanilla or caramel-apple
yogurt

½ medium apple, cored and
thinly sliced

2 pinches of ground
cinnamon, or to taste

Preheat the oven broiler.

Place the pita halves on a small nonstick baking sheet. Set the pan 6" from the heat source. Broil for 30 to 60 seconds per side, or until just warmed and barely toasted. Carefully open one pocket and spread 2 tablespoons of the yogurt evenly inside. Insert half of the apple slices evenly over the yogurt. Season with half of the cinnamon. Repeat with the other pita half, yogurt, apple, and cinnamon. Serve immediately.

Makes 1 serving

Per serving: 216 calories, 8 g protein, 45 g carbohydrates, 1 g fat (trace saturated), 3 mg cholesterol, 5 g fiber, 305 mg sodium

KELLY'S COTTAGE CHEESE AND FRUIT PARFAIT

Kelly MacFarland loves this go-to recipe as a breakfast or snack. Sometimes she also adds a layer (about ½ cup) of high-fiber cereal like Kashi or Grape-Nuts. "This gives it some crunch and it's really filling," she says. Actually, she loves it so much, she sometimes throws it in a big plastic cup to go.

1 green apple, cut into small chunks, divided

½ cup 1% cottage cheese

¼ cup blueberries

Place half of the apple chunks in a glass parfait dish or cereal bowl. Top evenly with half of the cottage cheese and the blueberries. Add the remaining cottage cheese and the remaining apple. Serve immediately.

Makes 1 serving

Per serving: **174 calories, 15 g protein, 27 g carbohydrates, 2 g fat (less than 1 g saturated), 5 mg cholesterol, 4 mg fiber, 461 mg sodium**

TRAINER TIP: **KIM LYONS**

To metabolize carbs more quickly, eat pastas and breads before 3:00 pm and only a few times weekly. Stick to veggies and proteins for late afternoon and dinner.

5

Hearty Snacks

Forget about what diet gurus used to tell you about not snacking between meals. New research has shown that snacking is a great weight-loss strategy—as long as you're not snacking on unhealthy junk food. The recipes in this chapter are so delicious, you won't miss those fat-filled and sodium-loaded potato chips. There is enormous wisdom in eating frequently, which is why healthy snacking is one of the hallmarks of a successful dieter. It just makes sense that if you eat more often, you'll be hungry less often—safeguarding you from unhealthy temptations.

In addition, snacking helps you tame carb and sugar cravings. It aids in controlling blood sugar and insulin levels (insulin is a fat-forming hormone) and leads to lower body fat. Best of all, it keeps you from feeling deprived and it allows you to be flexible in the way you eat. On the Biggest Loser diet, you get to snack from one to three times a day, depending on your daily calorie goals.

Snacks can be sweet or savory, but this chapter focuses on scrumptious recipes for hearty and savory snacks. When you're in the mood for something salty, need a protein boost, or want to fill up on fiber, snack time is the time to do it. If you're looking to snack on the go, try some of the yummy dips or the rollup recipes invented by the Biggest Losers themselves. Other recipes in this chapter are fit for entertaining; your guests won't have a clue that the Cocktail-Hour Tuna Tartare or Champ's Chicken Quesadilla are actually healthy dishes!

COCKTAIL-HOUR TUNA TARTARE

If you love sushi, you can't possibly go wrong with this fresh and light dish that I like to serve in a martini glass! Just be 100 percent sure that you buy sashimi- or sushi-grade tuna. When I quadruple this recipe for guests, I like to cut green onions into fine, long slivers and soak them in ice-cold water. Those pretty green onion curls are perfect for an elegant garnish—and your guests will never believe they're eating healthy.

4 ounces sashimi- or sushi-grade ahi tuna, finely chopped

2 tablespoons minced mango

1 tablespoon minced seeded cucumber

2 teaspoons lime juice, or more to taste

1 teaspoon chopped fresh cilantro leaves

1 teaspoon chopped green onion tops

½ teaspoon toasted sesame oil

¼ teaspoon hot sesame oil

Pinch of salt, or to taste

In medium bowl, combine the tuna, mango, cucumber, 2 teaspoons lime juice, cilantro, green onion, toasted sesame oil, hot sesame oil, and salt. Stir to mix. Taste and add up to 1 teaspoon more lime juice if desired. Spoon the mixture into a martini glass or mound onto a small serving plate.

Makes 1 serving

Per serving: 192 calories, 28 g protein, 5 g carbohydrates, 6 g fat (less than 1 g saturated), 0 mg cholesterol, less than 1 g fiber, 146 mg sodium

AMY HILDRETH

Take your favorite recipes and modify them so they're healthy. That way you won't feel as if you're denying yourself.

CHAMP'S CHICKEN QUESADILLA

Growing up in Pennsylvania and having a mother who made great American and Italian classics like meatloaf, spaghetti and meatballs, and burgers every week, I'm not sure I even knew what a quesadilla was as a teen. Imagine my shock when I moved to LA and client after client topped their "craving list" with quesadillas. Fortunately, I quickly realized that it's relatively easy to create a well-balanced healthy version . . . Phew!

¼ teaspoon chili powder

¼ teaspoon paprika

¼ teaspoon onion powder

Pinch of garlic powder

Pinch of ground cumin

Pinch of salt

2 ounces boneless, skinless chicken breast, trimmed of visible fat

1 whole-wheat flour, 96% fat-free tortilla (8" diameter)

½ cup (1 ounce) finely shredded Cabot 75% Light Cheddar Cheese

Preheat the grill to high heat. In a small bowl, combine the chili powder, paprika, onion powder, garlic powder, cumin, and salt. Rub the mixture evenly over the chicken. Cover with plastic wrap and refrigerate for 10 minutes, for flavors to blend.

Place the chicken on the grill and lower the heat to medium. (If it is not possible to reduce the heat, sear the chicken quickly on both sides and then move away from direct heat.) Grill the chicken for 2 to 4 minutes per side, or until it is no longer pink and the juices run clear. Set aside for about 10 minutes. Chop the chicken coarsely.

Preheat a medium nonstick skillet over medium heat. With an oven mitt, briefly remove it from the heat to mist with olive oil spray. Lay the tortilla in the pan. Cook for 30 seconds. Flip the tortilla. Evenly scatter cheese over half the tortilla. Top with the reserved chicken. With a spatula, fold the tortilla in half over the filling. Cook for 2 to 4 minutes, or until it starts to brown in spots. Flip and cook 2 to 4 minutes, or until the bottom starts to brown in spots and the cheese is melted. Slice into 4 wedges. Serve immediately.

Makes 1 serving

Per serving: **242 calories, 26 g protein, 25 g carbohydrates, 5 g fat (2 g saturated), 43 mg cholesterol, 3 g fiber, 454 mg sodium**

RYAN'S GROUND TURKEY NACHOS

Ryan Kelly fell in love with this dish while she was on the ranch. Though she sprays "each individual chip with I Can't Believe It's Not Butter! spray," I'd prefer to save the spray for popcorn or other blander snacks. She also bakes them and uses fat-free cheddar, but I prefer reduced-fat nacho cheese sauce so there is no need for baking. You can also add 1 teaspoon salt-free Mexican or Southwest seasoning to the turkey before cooking. Feel free to follow either of our suggestions or to tweak the dish even further to your own tastes.

1   ounce baked tortilla chips (about 20 chips)

3   ounces Jennie-O Turkey Store Extra Lean Ground Turkey

2   tablespoons canned fat-free refried beans

1   tablespoon reduced-fat nacho cheese sauce

2   tablespoons salsa, drained if watery

1   tablespoon fat-free sour cream

1   teaspoon minced chives

Arrange the chips in a medium shallow bowl.

Set a small skillet over medium-high heat until it is hot enough for a spritz of water to sizzle on it. With an oven mitt, briefly remove the pan from the heat to mist with olive oil spray. Set over medium-high heat and add the turkey. Cook, breaking into chunks with a wooden spoon, for 3 to 5 minutes, or until no longer pink. Reduce the heat to low. Stir in the beans.

Meanwhile, spoon the cheese sauce into a microwaveable bowl. Microwave on low power in 15-second intervals until it is warm.

Spoon the turkey mixture evenly over the reserved chips. Drizzle on the cheese sauce. Spoon on the salsa and sour cream. Sprinkle on the chives.

Makes 1 serving

Per serving: **285 calories, 28 g protein, 35 g carbohydrates, 4 g fat (less than 1 g saturated), 37 mg cholesterol, 4 g fiber, 522 mg sodium**

THIN-AND-CRISPY BBQ-CHICKEN PIZZA SNACK WEDGES

Yes! You can have pizza and eat healthy. And you don't have to feel guilty about it. I always serve this pizza at my Super Bowl parties and when I invite girlfriends over for TV nights. My friends always rave and swear there's no way it's low in fat. This recipe is particularly great for kids, too!

1 whole-wheat flour, 96% fat-free tortilla (8" diameter)

2 tablespoons barbecue sauce (7 grams carbs or less per 2 tablespoons)

½ cup (2 ounces) finely shredded Cabot 75% Light Cheddar Cheese

⅔ cup (3 ounces) chopped grilled chicken breast

¼ cup slivered red onion

1½ teaspoons chopped fresh cilantro leaves

Preheat the oven to 400°F.

Place the tortilla on a small nonstick baking sheet. Bake for 4 to 5 minutes per side, or until crisp. If air bubbles form, poke them with a fork, then press out the air with a spatula or oven mitt. Remove the sheet from the oven. Top the tortilla evenly in layers with the sauce, cheese, chicken, onion, and cilantro. Bake for 2 to 4 minutes, or until the cheese is completely melted. Slice into 8 wedges. Serve immediately.

Makes 1 serving

Per serving: 381 calories, 45 g protein, 32 g carbohydrates, 9 g fat (3 g saturated), 78 mg cholesterol, 3 g fiber, 861 mg sodium

It is critical that you do not attempt to make a pizza "crust" from a low-carb tortilla. It will smoke and burn, without becoming crisp.

Most barbecue sauce is high in sugar and carbohydrates. I always look for one with 7 grams or less of carbs per serving. Although you can use "low-carb" barbecue sauce, I have not found one that I enjoy, so I opt for one that contains less carbohydrates rather than one that's called "low-carb."

THIN-AND-CRISPY SAUSAGE AND MUSHROOM PIZZA

As a teen struggling to lose weight, I used to have two recurring nightmares. In one, I'd eat an entire cheesecake and in the other, I'd eat an entire pizza loaded with pepperoni and meatballs. At least once every month or so, I'd wake up in a cold sweat, realize I hadn't actually done that, and feel so relieved. Now, instead of dreaming about them, I indulge in much more sensible versions. This pizza is mounded with sausage for two reasons: for sheer taste and because it adds lean protein to an otherwise high-carbohydrate meal. So, take that, Sand Man.

1 whole-wheat flour, 96% fat-free tortilla (8" diameter)

⅓ cup sliced fresh mushrooms

¼ cup sauce from Superior Spaghetti and Meatballs (page 190) or jarred low-fat, low-sodium marinara sauce

½ cup (1 ounce) finely shredded, low-fat mozzarella cheese

1 recipe sausage from Individual Sausage-Rigatoni Bake (page 186)

Red-pepper flakes (optional)

Preheat the oven to 400°F.

Place the tortilla on a small nonstick baking sheet. Bake for 4 or 5 minutes per side, or until crisp. If air bubbles form, poke them with a fork, then use a spatula or oven mitt to press out the air.

Meanwhile, mist a small nonstick skillet with olive oil spray. Set over medium heat. Add the mushrooms. Cook, stirring occasionally, for about 5 minutes, or until tender. Set aside.

Top the tortilla evenly in layers with the sauce, cheese, reserved mushrooms, and sausage. Season with red-pepper flakes, if desired.

Bake for 2 to 4 minutes, or until cheese is completely melted. Slice into 4 wedges. Serve immediately.

Makes 1 serving

Per serving: **321 calories, 30 g protein, 33 g carbohydrates, 9 g fat (2 g saturated), 65 mg cholesterol, 5 g fiber, 626 mg sodium**

It is critical that you do not attempt to make a pizza "crust" from a low-carb tortilla. It will smoke and burn, without becoming crisp.

KEN'S KIMCHEE CUPS

Given Ken Coleman's big personality, it's no surprise that he loves big flavors. This extremely simple dish derives much of its flavor from pickled cabbage, which is found in jars, usually refrigerated, in most major grocery stores. This recipe has a great kick that creates the perfect flavor—and there's very little fat!

¼ pound boneless pork chop, trimmed of visible fat and cut into thin, 1"-long strips

¼ teaspoon Chinese five-spice powder

¼ teaspoon garlic powder

2 pinches of salt

4 leaves Bibb or Boston lettuce

½ cup cooked short-grain brown rice (reheated if using leftover rice)

⅓ cup kimchee (Korean pickled cabbage)

In a small bowl, combine the pork, five-spice powder, garlic powder, and salt. Toss to coat. Cover the bowl with plastic wrap. Refrigerate for at least 5 minutes for the seasonings to flavor the pork.

Place a small nonstick skillet over medium-high heat until it is hot enough for a spritz of water to sizzle on it. With an oven mitt, briefly remove the pan from the heat to mist lightly with olive oil spray. Add the pork. Cook, stirring occasionally, for 2 to 4 minutes, or until browned on all sides and no longer pink inside.

Place the lettuce leaves side by side on a serving plate. Fill the leaves with equal amounts of rice, pork, and kimchee. Serve immediately.

Makes 1 serving

Per serving: **266 calories, 29 g protein, 27 g carbohydrates, 4 g fat (1 g saturated), 62 mg cholesterol, 4 g fiber, 495 mg sodium**

GOURMET ROAST BEEF ROLLUPS

These rollups are a great appetizer to take to a party. Not only will you look like a star for bringing such attractive, tasty food, if everything else is fried (it's happened to me a lot!), you'll have something to munch on yourself. And you'll set yourself up to avoid unhealthy food without starving. Just be sure you use roast beef that's been shaved or is very thinly sliced; otherwise the tortillas will tear when you roll them. The chili garlic sauce is available in the international foods aisle of most major grocery stores with other Thai ingredients. If you can't find it, subbing in chili paste is okay, too.

1 tablespoon fat-free cream cheese

¼ to ½ teaspoon chili garlic sauce

1 whole-wheat flour, 96% fat-free tortilla (8" diameter)

Scant ¼ cup roasted red bell pepper strips

¼ cup loosely packed chopped fresh basil leaves

¾ cup (3 ounces) shaved Rosemary-Grilled London Broil (page 159) or lean, low-sodium deli roast beef

In a small bowl, combine the cream cheese and chili garlic sauce to taste. Stir to mix well. Place the tortilla on a cutting board. Spread the cheese mixture evenly over about two-thirds of the tortilla to the edges. Top the cream cheese mixture with the pepper strips, basil, and roast beef. Starting at the filled end, roll the tortilla tightly into a tube, being careful not to tear it.

Space 8 toothpicks evenly across it and poke them into the tube so they go through and touch the cutting board. With a sharp knife, cut between the picks to make 8 pieces. Take one piece and push the toothpick through so that the roll is evenly spaced in the center. Repeat with the remaining pieces. Arrange, spiral side up, on a serving plate. Serve immediately or cover with plastic wrap and refrigerate for up to 6 hours.

Makes 1 serving

Per serving: 226 calories, 22 g protein, 30 g carbohydrates, 5 g fat (1 g saturated), 35 mg cholesterol, 3 g fiber, 409 mg sodium

Just ¼ cup of most jarred roasted bell pepper strips has about 300 milligrams of sodium, so it is best to roast fresh peppers yourself if at all possible. For instructions, see Roasted Red Pepper Dip (page 85).

KELLY'S TURKEY ROLLUPS

We all fell in love with Kelly Minner in season one when she took the top spot, becoming the Biggest Loser among the ladies. All the while, she was falling in love with her new favorite snack, these turkey rollups. Kelly especially likes this recipe when it's made with smoked turkey, but if you're watching your sodium intake, you can use leftovers from the BBQ Turkey Breast Roast (page 175) or store-bought turkey, as we do below.

1 whole wheat flour, low-carb tortilla (7½" diameter)

1 tablespoon light garden vegetable cream cheese

2 ounces thinly sliced lower-sodium oven-roasted turkey

Place the tortilla on a cutting board. Spread the cream cheese evenly over three-quarters of the tortilla surface to the edges. Lay the turkey slices evenly over the cheese. Starting at the filled end, roll the tortilla tightly into a tube. With a sharp knife, slice into 8 equal pieces. Arrange, spiral side up, on a serving dish. Serve immediately.

Makes 1 serving

Per serving: 130 calories, 17 g protein, 8 g carbohydrates, 3 g fat (less than 1 g saturated), 28 mg cholesterol, 3 g fiber, 720 mg sodium

TRAINER TIP: BOB HARPER

When it comes to feeling self-conscious at the gym, we've all been there. You need to focus on what you need to do. Find *your* gym. Find one thing that you can do at that gym. Take care of yourself, and then just go on through the rest of your day.

JESSICA'S "THE RANCH" BLT WRAP

Jessica Lanham has always been a huge fan of BLTs. When she got to the ranch she learned that she "could still have them, but with a twist." Do note, however, that though this version contains much less fat and calories than a traditional BLT, it is still very high in sodium. To achieve maximum weight-loss results, you might want to indulge in this treat only from time to time—when you're really craving a BLT.

3 strips nitrate-free turkey bacon

1 whole-wheat flour, low-carb tortilla (7½" diameter)

1 tablespoon Galeo's Miso Caesar Dressing (optional)

2 small leaves green leaf lettuce

3 very thin slices tomato

Set a medium nonstick skillet over medium-high heat until it is hot enough for a spritz of water to sizzle on it. Place the bacon in the pan. Cook, flipping several times, for 4 to 6 minutes, or until crisp. Transfer to a plate and cover to keep warm. Place the tortilla in the pan. Cook for about 30 seconds per side, or until just warmed.

Transfer the tortilla to a serving plate. Spread half of it evenly with the Caesar dressing, if desired. Top the Caesar dressing with the lettuce leaves. Lay the reserved bacon strips side by side over the lettuce. Top with the tomato. Starting from the filled end, roll into a tube. Serve immediately.

Makes 1 serving

Per serving: **187 calories, 23 g protein, 10 g carbohydrates, 7 g fat (less than 1 g saturated), 75 mg cholesterol, 4 g fiber, 870 mg sodium**

PB&J SPIRALS

I dated a guy who loved peanut butter and jelly. One day just when I'd thrown the last slice of bread into the food processor for bread crumbs, he came home ready for a quick PB&J sandwich between appointments. I felt bad, so I offered to make him something, but he didn't think he had enough time to wait. In a pinch, I threw the PB&J on a tortilla. He looked at me like I was nuts and ran out the door with it. The next morning, I caught him making another one—and I'd already restocked the bread. This recipe is a bit higher in fat than most in the book, but most of the fat comes from peanut butter, which provides good fat. Just be sure to alternate this with higher-fiber, lower-fat snacks.

1   whole-wheat flour, low-carb, tortilla (7½" diameter)

1½ tablespoons reduced-fat peanut butter

1   tablespoon 100% strawberry all-fruit spread (or your favorite flavor)

Set a medium nonstick skillet over medium heat for about 1 minute, or until hot. Place the tortilla in the skillet. Cook for 20 to 30 seconds per side, or until just warm.

Place the tortilla on a cutting board. Spread the surface evenly with the peanut butter followed by the fruit spread. Roll into a tube. Slice into 8 equal pieces. Arrange on a serving plate, spiral side up. Serve immediately.

Makes 1 serving

Per serving: 253 calories, 10 g protein, 28 g carbohydrates, 12 g fat (2 g saturated), 0 mg cholesterol, 5 g fiber, 448 mg sodium

ERIK'S VEGGIE TUNA SNACK WRAPS

After giving up Porterhouse steaks and full-fat lasagna, Erik Chopin found this hearty wrap to be a saving grace. He loves the flavor of the fiber-packed tuna treasure so much, he's added it to the menu in the deli he owns in New York City. He sometimes skips the vinaigrette and opts for red wine vinegar spiked with Splenda, which saves 20 calories and 1 to 2 grams of fat per wrap.

2 broccoli florets

1 can (6 ounces) reduced-sodium, chunk light tuna in water, drained

1 tablespoon finely chopped red bell pepper

1 tablespoon finely chopped yellow bell pepper

1 tablespoon finely chopped green bell pepper

1 tablespoon finely chopped red onion

1 tablespoon light red wine vinaigrette

1 tablespoon spicy brown mustard, or to taste

2 whole-wheat flour, low-carb tortillas (7½" diameter)

½ cup loosely packed fresh spinach leaves

In a small saucepan, bring 2 cups of water to a boil over high heat. Add the broccoli. Cook for 1 minute, or until crisp-tender. Drain and rinse under cold water to cool completely. Pat dry. Chop finely. Transfer to a medium bowl. Add the tuna, bell peppers, and onion. Toss to mix. Add the vinaigrette and 1 tablespoon mustard. Toss to mix well. Taste and add more mustard, if desired.

Place one tortilla on a serving plate. Spoon half of the tuna mixture over two-thirds of the tortilla. Arrange half of the spinach leaves evenly over the tuna mixture. Starting at the filled end, roll the tortilla tightly into a tube. Repeat with the remaining tortilla, tuna mixture, and spinach. Serve immediately.

Makes 2 servings

Per serving: **217 calories, 22 g protein, 23 g carbohydrates, 4 g fat (less than 1 g saturated), 38 mg cholesterol, 12 g fiber, 647 mg sodium**

The wraps can be prepared in advance. Wrap them in plastic wrap and refrigerate for up to 24 hours.

PAM'S COTTAGE CHEESE MARINARA

Always a fan of lasagna, Pam Smith wanted the taste without all the carbs. She decided to skip the noodles and started eating the low-fat ricotta and mozzarella filling mixed with some marinara sauce. She got hooked. One night on the ranch when the craving struck, she found that someone else had finished the ricotta cheese, but there was still some fat-free cottage cheese in the fridge. "So I decided to improvise," says Pam, "and it tasted great. Plus, it's so quick and easy, it's hard to go wrong."

½ cup fat-free cottage cheese

2½ tablespoons (½ ounce) finely shredded low-fat mozzarella cheese

¼ cup Superior Spaghetti Sauce (page 191) or other low-fat, low-sugar, low-sodium marinara sauce

In a small, microwaveable bowl, combine the cottage cheese, mozzarella, and sauce. Stir to mix. Microwave on medium power for 1 to 2 minutes, or until the mozzarella is melted and the mixture is hot. Serve immediately.

Makes 1 serving

Per serving: **146 calories, 18 g protein, 14 g carbohydrates, 2 g fat (less than 1 g saturated), 10 mg cholesterol, 2 g fiber, 615 mg sodium**

KIMMI AND BRUCE'S CHICKEN LETTUCE WRAPS

Engaged couple Kimmi Dove and Bruce Lebowsky (and I) love the combo of flavors and kick in these wraps. There are a lot of ingredients, so the recipe might look intimidating, but it is really quite easy and well worth making. If you're not a spicy food lover, you may want to start with a teaspoon of hot sauce instead of the 2 teaspoons.

1 can (8 ounces) bamboo shoots, drained and minced

1 can (8 ounces) water chestnuts, drained and minced

3 tablespoons sherry

2 tablespoons hoisin sauce

1 tablespoon unsalted freshly ground peanut butter or reduced-fat peanut butter

2 teaspoons low-sodium soy sauce

2 teaspoons hot-pepper sauce

2 packets (.035 ounce each) sugar substitute (such as Splenda)

1 tablespoon minced garlic

1 cup minced onion

½ pound ground chicken breast

2 teaspoons minced fresh ginger

In a medium bowl, combine the bamboo shoots, water chestnuts, sherry, hoisin sauce, peanut butter, soy sauce, hot-pepper sauce, and sugar substitute. Mix well. Set aside.

Mist a large, nonstick skillet with olive oil spray and set over medium heat. Add the garlic and cook for 2 minutes, or until fragrant. Add the onion. Cook, stirring occasionally, for 3 to 4 minutes, or until tender and just starting to brown. Increase the heat to medium-high. Add the chicken, ginger, and salt. Cook, breaking the chicken into small chunks, for 3 to 4 minutes, or until no longer pink. Add the reserved bamboo shoot mixture. Cook for 2 minutes, or until hot. Stir in the sesame oil. Remove the pan from the heat. Spoon the chicken mixture, evenly divided, into the lettuce leaves. Set on a serving dish. Top with green onion and cucumber. Serve immediately.

Makes 4 (2-wrap) servings

¼ teaspoon salt

1 teaspoon toasted sesame
oil

8 small leaves butter lettuce

1 whole green onion,
chopped

1 small cucumber, seeded
and sliced into 1" strips

Per serving: 191 calories, 16 g protein, 22 g carbohydrates, 4 g fat (less than 1 g saturated), 33 mg cholesterol, 5 g fiber, 637 mg sodium

LOX-OF-MUSCLE CRISPS

A number of contestants approached me about creating a dish that would satisfy their cravings for smoked salmon—bagels and lox is a Sunday brunch favorite. The problem, however, is that lox tends to have over 2,000 milligrams of sodium in a 4-ounce serving. The brands found at my local grocery stores even exceeded 2,500 milligrams, which means that a mere ounce has over 550 milligrams. Here is a throw-together substitute that still gives you the essence of that great smoky taste without sending your blood pressure soaring.

2 tablespoons fat-free cream cheese

2 teaspoons chopped fresh dill

½ ounce smoked salmon, minced

2 Fat-Free RyKrisp Crackers

1 teaspoon minced red onion

In a small bowl, combine the cream cheese and dill. Mix well. Gently stir in the salmon.

Spread half of the salmon mixture evenly over each cracker. Place on a serving plate. Sprinkle half of the onion over each cracker. Serve immediately.

Makes 1 serving

Per serving: 95 calories, 8 g protein, 13 g carbohydrates, 1 g fat (trace saturated), 6 mg cholesterol, 3 g fiber, 507 mg sodium

TRAINER TIP: **KIM LYONS**

Keep in mind that the scale does not show water weight or muscle gain. Go by how you clothes fit and, if you can, get your body composition tested.

WARM CRAB SPREAD WITH CRACKERS

I spent years being crabby on diets. I'd carry around carrots sticks and take containers of tuna to the middle school cafeteria—only to get picked on for eating "weird" food, even though I hated every minute of it. I even managed to go an entire year without eating chocolate, but I was secretly angry and envious the whole time. I was so much less happy than I am today. So as a tribute to those crabby days being long gone, here's a crabby dish that's much more enjoyable than I must have been in my days of deprivation.

1 tub (8 ounces) fat-free cream cheese, at room temperature

1 can (6.5 ounces) lump crab meat, drained

1 whole green onion, finely chopped

1 teaspoon prepared horseradish

1 teaspoon Worcestershire sauce

⅛ teaspoon hot-pepper sauce

8 Fat-Free RyKrisp Crackers

Preheat the oven to 375°F. Mist four 3"-diameter ovenproof ramekins or custard cups with olive oil spray.

In a small mixing bowl, beat the cream cheese with an electric mixer until smooth. Add the crab meat, green onion, horseradish, Worcestershire sauce, and hot-pepper sauce. Stir with a spatula to mix well. Spoon into the prepared ramekins or cups.

Bake for 12 to 14 minutes, or until heated through. Remove and set aside for about 5 minutes to cool slightly. Serve each ramekin or cup with 2 crackers.

Makes 4 servings

Per serving: 138 calories, 16 g protein, 15 g carbohydrates, 1 g fat (less than 1 g saturated), 32 mg cholesterol, 3 g fiber, 491 mg sodium

AMY'S SMOTHERED CREAM CHEESE SPREAD

Amy Hildreth is a class act all the way and she is now determined to eat and serve food that follows. Whether it is having girlfriends over to watch The Biggest Loser *or throwing fancy cocktail parties, Amy always impresses. Now she is working on creating healthier party fare. This twist on a very simple but elegant appetizer is one of her new favorites—especially when served with Fat-Free RyKrisp Crackers, Wasa Light Rye Crispbread, or other 100% whole wheat crackers.*

1 tub (8 ounces) fat-free cream cheese

⅓ cup 100% fruit spread, any flavor

With a butter knife, scrape around the inside wall of the tub to loosen the cream cheese. Flip the tub onto a dessert plate to unmold the cream cheese. If it doesn't fall out, use a spoon to scoop it out, trying to keep it as intact as possible. If any cheese sticks to the tub, evenly spread it over the mound and smooth it with a knife. Spoon the fruit spread over the cheese.

Makes 8 (2½-tablespoon) servings

Per serving: 52 calories, 4 g protein, 8 g carbohydrates, 0 g fat, 4 mg cholesterol, 0 g fiber, 172 mg sodium

ERIK CHOPIN

Instead of watching the clock during cardio workouts, listen to music.

SPINACH SKINNY-DIP

This is another recipe that I never hesitate to dish up at parties. It's great served in a hollowed-out whole-grain bread bowl and people always swear, "It's too good to be virtually fat-free." Whether you're enjoying it as an afternoon snack for yourself or serving it to impress guests, be sure to have plenty of fresh cut-up veggies on hand and always serve it chilled.

---

1 package (10 ounces) frozen chopped spinach, thawed

⅔ cup drained sliced water chestnuts

3 whole green onions

2 cloves garlic

½ cup fat-free sour cream

½ cup fat-free plain yogurt

½ teaspoon prepared hot mustard

Salt, to taste

Ground black pepper, to taste

Place the spinach in the center of a clean dishtowel. Fold the towel over the spinach and squeeze out as much moisture as possible. (This is important so the dip won't be watery.) Set aside.

In a food processor fitted with a chopping blade, combine the water chestnuts, green onions, and garlic. Process until the mixture is finely chopped. Add the spinach. Process for 10 seconds, or until combined. Add the sour cream, yogurt, and mustard. Season with salt and pepper. Process for 30 seconds, or until smooth. Transfer to a serving bowl. Cover with plastic wrap. Refrigerate for at least 1 hour before serving.

Makes 18 (2-tablespoon) serving.

Per serving: 21 calories, 1 g protein, 4 g carbohydrates, trace fat (trace saturated), less than 1 mg cholesterol, less than 1 g fiber, 33 mg sodium

ROASTED RED PEPPER DIP

My friend Liza is obsessed with Moroccan food. I created this dip for her when she was trying to lose her "pregnancy weight." The strong cumin flavor coupled with the roasted bell peppers and creamy cheese was just what she needed to help her drop those frustrating 30 pounds. She chomped on tons of carrots and cucumber sticks dripping with it. I happen to love it as a spread in my wraps or served with shrimp, cubes of whole-grain bread, or Wasa Light Rye Crispbread.

3 large red bell peppers

2 whole green onions, cut into 2" lengths

2 tablespoons fresh cilantro leaves

2 large cloves garlic

1 tub (8 ounces) fat-free cream cheese, cut into pieces

½ cup seeded and chopped tomatoes

1 teaspoon ground cumin

Pinch of hot-pepper sauce, or to taste

Salt, to taste

Ground black pepper, to taste

Preheat the broiler or barbecue grill to high heat. With a small sharp knife, cut a couple of slits in the top of each bell pepper. Place the peppers on the rack 6" from the broiler heat source or on the grill rack. Cook for 2 to 5 minutes, or until the skin is charred black. Rotate the peppers so that another side faces the heat. Continue cooking until all sides are charred. Transfer the peppers to a brown paper bag. Close the bag tightly. Let stand for about 15 minutes, or until the peppers are cool enough to handle. One at a time, with hands, peel the charred skin from the peppers. Discard the skin, stem, and seeds.

Transfer the roasted peppers to the bowl of a food processor fitted with a chopping blade. Process for a few seconds, or until the peppers are roughly chopped. Spoon the peppers into a fine strainer or sieve. Stir to allow the excess liquid to drain off.

Meanwhile, to the bowl of the food processor, add the green onions, cilantro, and garlic. Process for about 60 seconds, or until finely chopped. Add the cream cheese. Process for about 60 seconds, or until well combined. Transfer the mixture to a medium bowl. Stir in the reserved bell peppers, tomatoes, and cumin. Stir to mix well. Season with hot-pepper sauce, salt, and black pepper. Cover the bowl. Refrigerate for at least 3 hours or up to 2 days, for the flavors to blend.

Makes about 18 (2-tablespoon) servings

Per serving: **22 calories, 2 g protein, 3 g carbohydrates, trace fat (trace saturated), 1 mg cholesterol, 1 g fiber, 72 mg sodium**

JEN'S ASPARAGUS GUACAMOLE

Former beauty pageant winner Jennifer Eisenbarth says that her guacamole is "the perfect dip for low-fat tortilla chips, your favorite veggies, or as a spread on wraps and sandwiches." In fact, this recipe is especially good in Matt's "Slap It Together" Turkey Guac-Sandwich (page 110). Jen suggests adding fresh cilantro, minced garlic, jalapeño, or other fresh ingredients to boost the flavor even further.

6 large spears fresh asparagus, ends trimmed, cut into 2" lengths

½ cup fat-free sour cream

2½ tablespoons guacamole seasoning mix

1 medium tomato, seeded and chopped

Bring 2 cups of water to a boil in a medium saucepan set over high heat. Place the asparagus in the pan. Boil for 3 to 5 minutes, or until tender. Drain and rinse under cold water to cool completely. Pat dry.

Place the asparagus in the bowl of a food processor fitted with a chopping blade. Process for 30 to 60 seconds, or until smooth. Add the sour cream and seasoning. Process for 30 seconds, or until smooth.

Transfer the mixture to a medium, airtight plastic container. Stir in the tomato. Mix until well combined. Refrigerate for at least 2 hours or up to 2 days for the flavors to blend.

Makes about 11 (2-tablespoon) servings

Per serving: **23 calories, less than 1 g protein, 4 g carbohydrates, trace fat (trace saturated), 1 mg cholesterol, trace fiber, 187 mg sodium**

BOB'S POPCORN WITH A JESSICA TWIST

The Navy wives were craving a snack one night at the ranch. "So I got out the popper and went to town," says Jessica Lanham. "The Navy wives loved it!" It is important to remember, however, that there is a significant amount of oil in the spray—there are 904 servings per bottle! If you use more than five or so spritzes, it does have calories and fat. For a Chef Devin twist, skip the Parmesan and garlic powder and opt for Cabot's Cheddar Shake. Two teaspoons have only 25 calories and 1½ grams of fat.

3 tablespoons plain popcorn kernels

I Can't Believe It's Not Butter! spray

2 teaspoons reduced-fat Parmesan cheese

4 pinches of garlic powder

In a hot-air popcorn popper or microwave, pop the kernels following the package directions. Transfer to a large bowl.

Spray the popcorn with 5 spritzes of I Can't Believe It's Not Butter! spray. Toss to coat. Repeat spraying and tossing four times for a total of 25 spritzes. Spritz 5 times and sprinkle with ½ teaspoon of cheese and a pinch of garlic powder. Toss the popcorn. Repeat, spritzing and sprinkling seasonings three more times, until all of the remaining cheese and garlic powder is used. (That's a total of 40 spritzes. It seems like a lot of work, but it's the best way to make the toppings stick to the popcorn.)

Makes 2 servings

Per serving: **74 calories, 2 g protein, 14 g carbohydrates, 1 g fat (0 g saturated), 3 mg cholesterol, 3 g fiber, 98 mg sodium**

6

Sandwiches, Soups, and Stews

The dishes in this chapter are rib-sticking, soul-satisfying, and downright comforting. After just one bite, you'll forget that you're eating healthy "diet" food. Soups, stews, and sandwiches lend themselves to healthful preparations without much change in flavor, texture, or pizzazz. Instead of a fatty burger with ground beef, try substituting ground turkey or chicken, like we did for the Creole Turkey Burger.

As you can tell from the recipes here, soups, stews, and sandwiches are really quite versatile. You can make them plain or fancy, you can serve them for lunch or dinner, and they're good in hot weather as well as cold. They also offer plenty of room for culinary creativity. Feel free to personalize these recipes by adding herbs, spices, or your favorite vegetables (as long as they're healthy, of course).

Best of all, these dishes will take you on a trip around the globe without leaving your kitchen. Every country in the world seems to have an exciting soup, stew, and sandwich repertoire. Check out our Pork and Black-Bean Verde Stew, Asian Meatball Soup, Quick and Easy Open Burrito, and good ol' American BBQ Pork Sandwich for a world-wide selection of flavors!

ALMOST FAST FOOD BURGER

If those drive-thru burgers call your name, this is, hands down, definitely the burger for you! As a kid and teen, I was addicted to fast food, so I was determined to recreate those drive-thru flavors and secret sauces at home. This burger is much, much leaner than any you're likely to find at a fast food restaurant, but the sauce makes it taste so reminiscent of them. I often make this burger in a low-carb tortilla instead of a hamburger bun and I always add a few more pickles. If you're watching your sodium closely, you may not want to stick to it "as is" below.

1 tablespoon low-fat mayonnaise

½ teaspoon ketchup

½ teaspoon yellow mustard

¼ pound 96% lean ground beef

1 slice (¾ ounce) fat-free American cheese (optional)

1 whole-grain or whole-wheat hamburger bun

¼ cup chopped romaine lettuce leaves

1 thin slice red onion

3 dill pickle rounds

In a small bowl, combine the mayonnaise, ketchup, and mustard. Stir to mix. Set aside. Shape the beef into a patty that is about ½" wider than the bun.

Preheat a medium nonstick skillet or grill rack on high heat. Place the patty on the pan or grill. Cook for 1 to 2 minutes per side, or until desired doneness. (Do not smash the burger with the spatula.) About 30 seconds before the burger is cooked, top with the cheese, if desired. Place the bun halves, cut sides down, on the pan or grill. Cook for about 45 seconds, or until toasted.

Place the bun bottom on a serving plate. Top with the patty, lettuce, onion, and pickles. Spread the reserved sauce evenly over the inside of the bun top. Flip onto the burger. Serve immediately.

Makes 1 serving

Per serving: **281 calories, 26 g protein, 27 g carbohydrates, 9 g fat (2 g saturated), 60 mg cholesterol, 4 g fiber, 736 mg sodium**

CALIFORNIA BACON BURGER

Bacon lovers, rejoice. This highly seasoned bacon burger is one of my favorites. True, it's a bit high in sodium, but worth every bite if your diet isn't otherwise full of sodium. I alternate making it with extra-lean ground beef and turkey and encourage you to swap in and out ingredients to your taste . . . as long as you're sticking to lean ones. The tablespoon of egg substitute and bread crumbs help to achieve the texture of a fattier burger.

1 strip nitrate-free turkey bacon, cut in half

1 tablespoon egg substitute

1 tablespoon Ian's Whole Wheat Panko Breadcrumbs or finely crushed Wasa Light Rye Crispbread

¼ pound Jennie-O Turkey Store Extra-Lean Ground Turkey

1 tablespoon chopped fresh parsley leaves

1 teaspoon Worcestershire sauce

1 teaspoon minced fresh jalapeño chile pepper

¾ ounce very thinly sliced Cabot's 75% Light Cheddar Cheese

1 whole-grain or whole-wheat hamburger bun

1 tablespoon low-fat mayonnaise

3 tomato slices, or to taste

1 thin slice red onion, or to taste

Place a medium nonstick pan over medium-high heat. Place the bacon in the pan. Cook for 3 to 4 minutes per side, or until crisp. Transfer to a plate. Cover to keep warm.

Meanwhile, in a small bowl, combine the egg substitute and bread crumbs or crushed crispbread. Add the turkey, parsley, Worcestershire sauce, and chile pepper. With clean hands or a fork, mix well. Shape into a patty that is about ½" wider than the bun.

Return the pan to medium-high heat until it is hot enough for a spritz of water to sizzle on it. With an oven mitt, briefly remove the pan from the heat to mist lightly with olive oil spray. Place the patty in the pan. Cook for about 2 minutes per side. Reduce the heat to medium. Cook for 2 minutes. Flip the patty. Cover it with cheese. Place the bun halves, cut side down, in the pan next to the patty. Cook for about 2 minutes, or until the turkey is no longer pink and the bun halves are toasted.

Place the bun bottom on a serving plate. Spread half of the mayonnaise over it. Top with the patty, bacon, tomato, and onion. Spread the remaining mayonnaise over the inside of the bun top. Flip onto the burger. Serve immediately.

Makes 1 serving

Per serving: 371 calories, 47 g protein, 27 g carbohydrates, 10 g fat (2 g saturated), 78 mg cholesterol, 2 g fiber, 832 mg sodium

CREOLE TURKEY BURGER

When making turkey burgers, I always use extra-lean ground turkey, then add moisture so I don't miss the fat. I also always mix seasonings into the meat before cooking it to give it added flavor. Here, I add a tablespoon of egg substitute and a tablespoon of bread crumbs to achieve the texture of a fattier burger. In other recipes, I sometimes opt for adding cooked brown rice which also softens the turkey. Ground turkey is also great when finished off with a seasoning blend or rub, as I did in this recipe. The Cajun seasoning goes quite well with the Creole mustard.

1 tablespoon low-fat mayonnaise

½ teaspoon Creole mustard

1 tablespoon egg substitute

1 tablespoon Ian's Whole Wheat Panko Breadcrumbs or finely crushed Wasa Light Rye Crispbread

¼ pound Jennie-O Turkey Store Extra Lean Ground Turkey

½ teaspoon Cajun seasoning

1 whole-grain or whole-wheat hamburger bun

1 leaf green leaf lettuce

1 slice tomato

In a small bowl, combine the mayonnaise and mustard. Stir to mix. Set aside.

In a second small bowl, combine the egg substitute and bread crumbs or crushed crispbread. Add the turkey and seasoning. With clean hands or a fork, mix well. Shape the mixture into a patty that is about ½" wider than the bun.

Set a medium nonstick skillet over medium-high heat until it is hot enough for a spritz of water to sizzle on it. Place the patty in the pan. Cook for 2 minutes per side, or until browned. Reduce the heat to medium and cook until it is no longer pink. Lay the bun halves, cut sides down, in the pan next to the patty. Cook for 1 to 2 minutes, or until toasted.

Place the bun bottom on a serving plate. Top with the patty, lettuce, and tomato. Spread the reserved mayonnaise mixture over the inside of the bun top. Flip onto the burger. Serve immediately.

Makes 1 serving

Per serving: **288 calories, 34 g protein, 29 g carbohydrates, 6 g fat (less than 1 g saturated), 45 mg cholesterol, 4 g fiber, 673 mg sodium**

SEXY JOES

From the time I was very young, I've been a huge fan of sloppy joes. This one is much leaner than most, and it's one of my all-time favorite versions. I prefer making this recipe with chicken over turkey, though both will work. If you have trouble finding extra-lean ground chicken, ask your butcher to grind chicken breasts for you. I've found that butchers at most major grocery stores will happily do it at no extra charge. Chicken breasts tend to cost less per pound that extra-lean ground chicken or turkey, so you may even save a few dollars.

---

1   pound extra-lean ground chicken

1   tablespoon white vinegar

2   teaspoons Worcestershire sauce

1½ teaspoons honey

½   teaspoon hot-pepper sauce

⅔   cup chopped yellow onion

⅓   cup chopped green bell pepper

¾   cup low-sodium tomato sauce

¾   cup chili sauce

¼   teaspoon chili powder

4   whole-grain or whole-wheat hamburger buns

Mist a medium nonstick skillet with olive oil spray and set it over medium-high heat. Add the chicken. Cook, stirring with a wooden spoon, breaking into large chunks, for 4 to 6 minutes, or until no longer pink.

Meanwhile, in a small bowl, combine the vinegar, Worcestershire, honey, and hot-pepper sauce. Whisk to blend. Set aside.

Drain off any liquid that has accumulated in the pan. Add the onion, bell pepper, tomato sauce, chili sauce, chili powder, and the reserved vinegar mixture to the pan. Stir to blend. Bring the mixture to a boil then reduce the heat so mixture simmers. Cook for 20 minutes, or until the mixture is thickened.

Spoon the mixture equally onto the opened buns. Serve immediately.

Makes 4 servings

Per serving: 331 calories, 31 g protein, 43 g carbohydrates, 4 g fat (less than 1 g saturated), 66 mg cholesterol, 5 g fiber, 876 mg sodium

QUICK AND EASY OPEN BURRITO

Using a large tortilla tends to add too many calories to a meal-sized burrito. Instead of skimping on the chicken, I like to make "open wraps." This open burrito is pick-up-able like a burrito and is as quick to make as a burrito—but it has a much better protein-to-carb ratio and is just as tasty.

¼ pound boneless, skinless chicken breast, trimmed of visible fat and thinly sliced

½ teaspoon extra-virgin olive oil

½ teaspoon paprika

⅛ teaspoon onion powder

⅛ teaspoon garlic powder

Pinch of ground cumin

Pinch of salt

Pinch of cayenne pepper

1 whole-wheat flour, 96% fat-free tortilla (8" diameter)

2 teaspoons fat-free sour cream

½ cup (1 ounce) finely shredded Cabot 75% Light Cheddar Cheese

¼ cup shredded romaine lettuce leaves

¼ cup seeded and chopped tomato

1 to 2 tablespoons red taco sauce, to taste

In a medium bowl, combine the chicken, oil, paprika, onion powder, garlic powder, cumin, salt, and cayenne pepper. Toss well to coat the chicken. Cover with plastic wrap. Refrigerate for at least 10 minutes for the flavors to blend.

Place a medium nonstick skillet over medium-high heat until it is hot enough for a spritz of water to sizzle on it. Scatter the chicken into the pan. Cook, stirring occasionally, 3 to 5 minutes, or until lightly browned on all sides and no longer pink. Transfer the chicken to a plate. Cover to keep warm. Set aside. Set the pan over medium heat. Place the tortilla in the pan. Cook for 30 to 60 seconds per side, or until it is just warmed.

Place the tortilla on a serving plate. Spread the sour cream in a 3"-wide strip halfway down the center of the tortilla. Top the sour cream with the cheese, lettuce, tomato, and the reserved chicken. Drizzle on the taco sauce. Fold the tortilla sides over the filling to the center and then fold up the bottom. Serve immediately.

Makes 1 serving

Per serving: **338 calories, 38 g protein, 30 g carbohydrates, 8 g fat (2 g saturated), 73 mg cholesterol, 3 g fiber, 642 mg sodium**

PORTOBELLO SURPRISE WRAP

My assistant Stephanie loves mushroom-anything. Her bright blue eyes light up every time she so much as talks about them. If you love portobello mushrooms half as much as she does, you're likely to be pleasantly surprised by the scrumptious taste of this extremely simple wrap. Not only is it low in fat and calories, it's one of Stephanie's all-time favorites.

1 large portobello mushroom cap

1 wedge (¾ ounce) Laughing Cow Light Garlic & Herb cheese

Salt, to taste

Ground black pepper, to taste

1 teaspoon Worcestershire sauce

½ cup yellow onion strips

1 tablespoon balsamic vinegar

1 whole-wheat flour, low-carb tortilla (7½" diameter)

Place the mushroom cap, stemmed-side down, on a cutting board. Holding a knife parallel to the cutting board, slice the cap in half, creating two disks. Remove the top disk and spread the cheese over the bottom disk. Place the top disk on the bottom disk. Coat the cap all over with olive oil spray. Season with salt and pepper. Set the mushroom stemmed side up and drizzle the Worcestershire sauce into the gills.

Mist a small nonstick skillet with olive oil spray. Set over medium heat. Add the onion to the pan. Cook, stirring occasionally, for 2 minutes. Drizzle in the vinegar. Cook for 3 to 4 minutes, or until soft. Transfer the onion to a plate. Cover to keep warm. Place the reserved mushroom, stemmed side down, in the pan. Cook for 3 minutes, pressing gently with a spatula. Flip the mushroom and cook for 3 minutes, or until tender. Transfer the mushroom to the onion plate. Place the tortilla in the pan. Cook about 30 seconds per side.

Put the tortilla on a serving plate. Place the mushroom on one side of the tortilla. Top with the onion. Fold the bare end of the tortilla up over the filling, and then fold the sides of the tortilla over the center. Serve immediately.

Makes 1 serving

Per serving: 183 calories, 9 g protein, 24 g carbohydrates, 5 g fat (2 g saturated), 10 mg cholesterol, 5 g fiber, 593 mg sodium

CHICKEN CHEESE-STEAK WRAP

The key to creating the perfect chicken for this taste of home (to me) is to make sure the pan is hot and that it is large enough for the chicken to lay flat when pulled apart. This is particularly important when cooking without a lot of fat. A cold pan or a heap of chicken will prevent it from getting that great browned flavor and color. So turn up the heat like we do in Philly! Also, be sure to shave the chicken as thinly as possible. Starting with a chicken breast that weighs more than ¼ pound makes it easier to get ¼ pound of shaved chicken. I always buy extra and reserve the remainder for another recipe.

¼ pound boneless, skinless chicken breast, trimmed of visible fat

¼ cup onion slivers

1 whole-wheat flour, low-carb tortilla (7½" diameter)

1 wedge (¾ ounce) Laughing Cow Original Light Swiss cheese

1 tablespoon low-sodium ketchup

2 teaspoons sliced pickled hot chile peppers

Place the chicken on a cutting board. With a sharp knife at a 45° angle, cut into very thin slivers.

Set a medium nonstick skillet over medium-high heat until it is hot enough for a spritz of water to sizzle on it. Mist with olive oil spray. Place the onion and the reserved chicken in the pan. Cook, separating the chicken shavings with 2 wooden spoons or spatulas, for 2 minutes, or until evenly browned and no longer pink. Remove the pan from the heat. Set aside.

Meanwhile, place the tortilla between 2 damp paper towels. Microwave on low power in 10-second intervals until warmed.

Place the tortilla on a serving plate. Spread the cheese, leaving about 2" bare on one end, in an even strip (about 3" wide) running down the center of the tortilla. Top with the chicken mixture, the ketchup, and peppers. Fold the bare end of the tortilla up over the filling, and then fold the sides of the tortilla over the middle. Serve immediately.

Makes 1 serving

Per serving: 264 calories, 33 g protein, 17 g carbohydrates, 6 g fat (2 g saturated), 76 mg cholesterol, 4 g fiber, 620 mg sodium

INDIAN CHICKEN SALAD POCKETS

I'm a big fan of mixing low-fat mayonnaise with stronger flavors to give it the richness of a full-fat mayonnaise. Here, I've coupled low-fat mayo with curry paste, which is found in the international foods aisle in most major grocery stores. Just be sure you don't go crazy with these pastes in other dishes—most are insanely full of fat and sodium. But they also have very strong flavor, so in a dish like this—where ½ teaspoon does it—I absolutely love them and I suspect you will, too.

1½ tablespoons low-fat mayonnaise

1 teaspoon lime juice, preferably fresh squeezed

½ teaspoon curry paste

¾ cup (4 ounces) chopped grilled chicken breast

1½ tablespoons seeded, chopped cucumber

1½ tablespoons chopped red onion

1 whole-wheat pita (6½" diameter), cut in half

2 leaves green leaf lettuce

In a medium bowl, combine the mayonnaise, lime juice, and curry paste. Whisk to blend. Add the chicken, cucumber, and onion. Mix well.

Spoon the mixture evenly into the pita halves. Add the lettuce. Serve immediately.

Makes 2 servings

Per serving: **186 calories, 20 g protein, 16 g carbohydrates, 5 g fat (1 g saturated), 48 mg cholesterol, 2 g fiber, 304 mg sodium**

JENNIFER EISENBARTH

Start and end every meal with a glass of water. If you're too full at the end of the meal to drink the water, you know that you've eaten too much.

BBQ CHICKEN BREAST SANDWICH

I tend to stay away from most foods labeled "low-carb," as many of them have more chemicals than I like to consume. However, I always look for products that are naturally low in carbohydrates. At every grocery store I've recently visited, I've found a least one barbecue sauce with 7 grams of carbohydrates or less per 2-tablespoon serving (most tend to have a lot more). These are in addition to those labeled "low-carb," which usually have 3 to 5 grams carbohydrates per serving. Hands down, no questions asked, I think the extra couple grams of carbs are worth opting for the former.

1 small (¼-pound) boneless, skinless chicken breast, trimmed of visible fat

1 tablespoon barbecue sauce (7 grams carbs or less per 2 tablespoons)

1 whole-grain or whole-wheat hamburger bun

1 large leaf green leaf lettuce

2 thin slices tomato

1 thin slice red onion

2 teaspoons low-fat mayonnaise

Place the chicken breast on a cutting board. Cover with a sheet of waxed paper. With the smooth head of a meat mallet, pound the chicken from the center out, until it is a uniform ½" thickness. Transfer to a medium shallow bowl. Add the sauce. Turn the chicken to coat all sides. Cover the bowl with plastic wrap. Refrigerate for at least 10 minutes to marinate.

Preheat the grill to high heat. Place the chicken on the grill. Turn the heat to low. (If it is not possible to reduce the heat, sear the chicken quickly on both sides and then move away from direct heat.) Cook for 3 to 5 minutes per side, or until it is no longer pink inside and the juices run clear. About 1 minute before the breast is done, place the bun halves, cut sides down, on the grill to toast.

Place the bottom half of the bun, toasted side up, on a serving plate. Top with the chicken breast, lettuce, tomato, and onion. Spread the mayonnaise over the inside of the top half of the bun. Flip onto the sandwich. Serve immediately.

Makes 1 serving

Per serving: **283 calories, 31 g protein, 27 g carbohydrates, 5 g fat (1 g saturated), 66 mg cholesterol, 2 g fiber, 499 mg sodium**

ROAST BEEF SANDWICH WITH HORSERADISH MAYO

There's something about horseradish on a roast beef sandwich that just works so perfectly. By making this sandwich yourself with a lean cut of roast beef and low-fat mayonnaise, you still get that amazing combo, without paying too high of a caloric price. Who said you can't eat hearty foods and still be healthy?

1 tablespoon low-fat mayonnaise

1 teaspoon prepared horseradish

2 slices whole-grain sandwich bread

1 leaf green leaf lettuce

1 cup (¼ pound) shaved Rosemary-Grilled London Broil (page 159) or lean, low-sodium deli roast beef

4 small slices tomato

1 thin slice red onion

In a small bowl, combine the mayonnaise and horseradish. Stir to blend. Set aside.

Place one slice of bread on a serving plate. Top with the lettuce, beef, tomato, and onion. Spread the reserved mayonnaise mixture evenly over the second slice of bread. Flip atop the sandwich. Cut in halves or quarters. Serve immediately.

Makes 1 serving

Per serving: 312 calories, 32g protein, 33 g carbohydrates, 8 g fat (3 g saturated), 53 mg cholesterol, 5 g fiber, 543 mg sodium

LISA ANDREONE

Remember that even 5 minutes of exercise is better than nothing, so try to do something every day. Take the stairs at work, or park your car far away and walk to your building. Every little bit helps.

BBQ PORK SANDWICH

This sandwich requires very little prep, but an hour of cooking time. And it's well worth the wait! When choosing a barbecue sauce, I choose one that happens to be low in carbohydrates (7 grams or less per 2 tablespoons) as opposed to a "low-carb" one. The former tends to be rich in flavor without being overly sweet. If you like extra barbecue sauce, add an additional tablespoon just before serving.

1½ teaspoons whole-grain oat flour

⅛ teaspoon garlic powder

⅛ teaspoon salt

Pinch of black pepper

½ pound pork tenderloin, cut into ¾" cubes

1 teaspoon extra-virgin olive oil

⅓ cup orange juice, preferably fresh-squeezed

⅓ cup white vinegar

1 tablespoon hickory smoke flavoring

1 tablespoon barbecue sauce (7 grams carbs or less per 2 tablespoons), or more to taste

½ cup onion strips (optional)

2 whole-grain or whole-wheat hamburger buns

In a medium resealable plastic bag, combine the flour, garlic powder, salt, and pepper. Add the pork. Seal the bag and shake to evenly coat the cubes. Refrigerate for at least 15 minutes.

Preheat a medium nonstick saucepan over medium-high heat until it is hot enough for a spritz of water to sizzle on it. Add the oil. Scatter the pork cubes into the pan. Cook, turning as needed, for about 5 minutes, or until pork is browned on all sides. Reduce the heat to medium. Add the orange juice, vinegar, and smoke flavoring. When the mixture comes to a boil, reduce the heat to low so the mixture simmers. Cover the pan. Cook, stirring occasionally, for 1 hour, or until the pork is very tender. With a wooden spoon, shred the pork pieces and mix in the barbecue sauce.

If the onion is desired, 5 minutes before serving, coat a small nonstick skillet with olive oil spray. Set over medium heat. Add the onion. Cook, stirring occasionally, for about 5 minutes, or until tender.

Meanwhile, place the bun halves, cut sides down, in a medium nonstick skillet set over medium heat. Cook for 3 to 5 minutes, or until toasted. Place the bun bottoms on serving plates. Spoon half of the pork mixture onto each bun bottom. Top with onion and additional barbecue sauce if desired. Cover with the bun tops. Serve immediately.

Makes 2 servings

Per serving: **316 calories, 28 g protein, 27 g carbohydrates, 9 g fat (2 g saturated), 74 mg cholesterol, 2 g fiber, 510 mg sodium**

RYAN'S OPEN-FACED MEATBALL SANDWICH

Ryan Benson has always been one for big portions. Now, though, those portions include plenty of lean protein and veggies. "I loved the homemade meatballs we were introduced to on the ranch," he says. "By making an open-faced sandwich with them, I was able to eat plenty without needing too much bread." This recipe ensures that Ryan has a big portion of lean protein without eating too many carbs.

3 regular Muscling-Up Meatballs (page 188)

⅓ cup sauce from Superior Spaghetti and Meatballs (page 190) or other low-sugar, low-fat marinara sauce

1 whole-grain or whole-wheat hot dog bun

¼ cup (1 ounce) shaved low-fat mozzarella cheese

In a small microwaveable bowl, combine the meatballs and the sauce. Microwave on low power in 30-second intervals until warmed through.

Meanwhile, preheat a small nonstick skillet over medium heat. Place the bun, cut side down, in the pan. Cook for 3 to 5 minutes, or until toasted.

Place the bun, toasted side up, on a serving plate. Top evenly with the cheese and the meatballs. Spoon any remaining sauce on top. Serve immediately.

Makes 1 serving

Per serving: 377 calories, 36 g protein, 44 g carbohydrates, 7 g fat (2 g saturated), 59 mg cholesterol, 7 g fiber, 840 mg sodium

MATT'S "SLAP IT TOGETHER" TURKEY-GUAC SANDWICH

Matt Hoover loves this sandwich because you just "slap it together and eat it." It's a great choice when he's trying to fit in healthy meals between his job, his workouts, and spending time with his friends. If you're like me and not a fan of fat-free mayo, feel free to skip it. You'll save calories and 240 milligrams sodium.

2 slices whole-wheat sandwich bread

2 tablespoons prepared spicy guacamole

1 cup (4 ounces) thinly sliced BBQ Turkey Breast Roast (page 175) or other low-sodium, low-fat turkey breast

⅓ cup alfalfa sprouts

⅓ cup shredded romaine lettuce leaves

2 slices tomato

2 tablespoons fat-free mayonnaise (optional)

Place one slice of bread on a plate. Spread with the guacamole. Top with the turkey, sprouts, lettuce, and tomato.

Spread the mayonnaise, if desired, over the second slice of bread. Place on the sandwich.

Makes 1 serving

Per serving: **343 calories, 41 g protein, 34 g carbohydrates, 7 g fat (trace saturated), 54 mg cholesterol, 6 g fiber, 574 mg sodium**

TRAINER TIP: **BOB HARPER**

When it comes to losing weight it's all about calories in, energy out. I am a firm believer that you have got to count calories when it comes to losing weight.

NAPOLEON TURKEY SANDWICH

I love the combo of flavors in this Italian-influenced sandwich. The tomatoes and red pepper strips add moisture to make the sandwich more decadent. If you're buying turkey precooked at the grocery store, make sure that you buy low-sodium, not lower-sodium, turkey breast. Many popular brands of lower-sodium turkey breast still have 650 to 700 milligrams of sodium (or more) in each 4-ounce serving.

¼ cup loosely packed fresh basil leaves

1½ tablespoons low-fat mayonnaise

¼ teaspoon minced garlic

2 slices whole-grain or sprouted-grain sandwich bread

¾ cup (3 ounces) thinly sliced BBQ Turkey Breast Roast (page 175) or other low-sodium, low-fat turkey breast

¾ ounce thinly sliced low-fat mozzarella cheese

Several arugula or spinach leaves

4 slices tomato

¼ cup roasted red pepper strips from Roasted Red Pepper Dip (page 85)

1 or 2 very thin slices red onion

In a mini-food processor or by hand, chop the basil leaves very finely. Transfer to a small bowl and add the mayonnaise and garlic. Stir to mix. Set aside.

Place one slice of bread on a serving plate. Cover with the turkey, mozzarella, arugula or spinach, tomato, red pepper strips, and onion. Spread the reserved mayonnaise mixture over the second slice of bread. Place on the sandwich. Serve immediately.

Makes 1 serving

Per serving: 332 calories, 32 g protein, 35 g carbohydrates, 9 g fat (2 g saturated), 39 mg cholesterol, 6 g fiber, 752 mg sodium

MATT'S GRILLED CHEESE SANDWICH

Matt Kamont has always been a big fan of cheese. He says, "I love mac and cheese, grilled cheese, bacon-egg-and-cheese bagels . . . anything with cheese, really." When he got home from the ranch, he was really missing cheese. He was determined to find a way to eat a healthier version of his favorite foods so he didn't go crazy and binge. He went to the grocery store and picked up some light rye and light cheddar, and now he can indulge in one of his all-time favorites.

2 slices light rye bread

1½ ounces paper-thin slices Cabot 75% light Cheddar cheese

I Can't Believe It's Not Butter! spray

Place one slice of bread on a serving plate. Top evenly with the cheese and the remaining slice of bread.

Preheat a small nonstick pan over medium heat until it is hot enough for a spritz of water to sizzle on it. With an oven mitt, briefly remove the pan from the heat to mist lightly with I Can't Believe It's Not Butter! spray. Place the sandwich in the pan. Cook for 3 to 4 minutes, or until the bread is lightly browned. Carefully flip the sandwich. Cook for 3 to 4 minutes, or until the cheese is completely melted. Serve immediately.

Makes 1 serving

Per serving: **189 calories, 18 g protein, 19 g carbohydrates, 6 g fat (2 g saturated), 15 mg cholesterol, 6 g fiber, 490 mg sodium**

WYLIE'S TURKEY GOULASH

Mark Wylie had been the quintessential bachelor who loved bachelor foods "like BBQ ribs with all the fixin's, Chinese takeout of orange beef with combo fried rice, and ICE CREAMMMMMMMMMM," he chuckles. He's recently turned in those foods, though, for better bachelor bites. His turkey goulash "is perfect because I can make it on Sunday and just heat it up after work." Wylie suggests serving it over brown rice or by itself in a bowl, with a side of wheat crackers.

1½ cups chopped onions

1½ tablespoons minced garlic

1 pound Jennie-O Turkey Store Extra Lean Ground Turkey

1 can (15 ounces) no-salt-added kidney beans with liquid

1 medium yellow summer squash, cut into bite-size chunks

1 can (14½ ounces) stewed tomatoes

1 teaspoon chili powder

1 teaspoon salt-free extra-spicy seasoning mix, or more to taste

¾ teaspoon salt

¼ teaspoon cayenne

Lightly mist a medium nonstick pot with olive oil spray. Set over medium heat. Place the onions and garlic in the pot. Cook, stirring occasionally, for 6 to 7 minutes, or until the onion is tender. Transfer the onion mixture to a bowl and set aside.

Set the pot over medium-high heat until it is hot enough for a spritz of water to sizzle on it. With an oven mitt, briefly remove the pan from the heat to mist lightly with olive oil spray. Add the turkey to the pot. Cook, breaking into chunks with a wooden spoon, for about 5 minutes, until lightly browned. Add the beans with liquid, squash, tomatoes, chili powder, 1 teaspoon seasoning mix, salt, cayenne, and the reserved onion mixture. Bring the mixture to a boil. Cover the pot. Reduce the heat to low and simmer, stirring occasionally, for 35 to 40 minutes, or until the veggies are tender. Taste and add more spicy seasoning mix, if desired. Serve immediately.

Makes 4 (1½-cup) servings

Per serving: 265 calories, 37 g protein, 29 g carbohydrates, 2 g fat (trace saturated), 45 mg cholesterol, 10 g fiber, 756 mg sodium

Any leftovers may be refrigerated in covered plastic storage containers for up to 3 days.

ASIAN MEATBALL SOUP

Even though we recommend that you limit your sodium intake, this recipe just wasn't the same with no-salt-added chicken broth. Instead, I used lower-sodium broth. The sodium content is a little high, so make sure you watch the sodium you consume in other foods the days you enjoy this tasty soup. Also, in this recipe, I like the pasta's texture better when it's only cooked for 3 minutes, which differs from the cooking time you'll find on the package directions.

Soup

2 cans (14 ounces each) lower-sodium chicken broth

8 thin slices peeled fresh ginger

5 whole green onions, chopped

2 tablespoons low-sodium soy sauce

4 ounces (half of an 8-ounce box) Nutrition Kitchen Angel Hair Style Golden Whole Soybean Pasta

⅓ cup drained canned bamboo shoots

2 tablespoons lime juice, preferably fresh squeezed

1 tablespoon toasted sesame oil

2 teaspoons hoisin sauce

½ teaspoon chili paste, or to taste

½ cup bean sprouts

To prepare the soup: In a medium, nonstick soup pot, combine the broth, ginger, chopped green onions, and soy sauce. Set over high heat. When the mixture reaches a boil, reduce the heat to low. Cover the pot. Simmer for 30 minutes.

Meanwhile, to prepare the meatballs: Preheat the oven to 400°F. Lightly mist a medium, nonstick baking sheet with olive oil spray. Set aside.

In a medium mixing bowl, combine the pork, yellow or white onion, water chestnuts, carrot, green onion, sherry, egg white, and sesame oil. With clean hands or a fork, mix well. With a 1¼" cookie scoop (or 2 spoons) shape the mixture into 1¼" meatballs. Place the meatballs on the prepared baking sheet so they do not touch. Bake for 8 to 10 minutes, or until they are no longer pink. Remove and set aside.

To continue with the soup: Bring a large pot of lightly salted water to a boil. Break the pasta in half and add to the pot. Stir. Cook, stirring occasionally, for 3 minutes. Drain and rinse under cold running water. Set aside.

Remove the ginger from the broth mixture and discard. Increase the heat to high. Add the bamboo shoots, lime juice, sesame oil, hoisin, chili paste, and the reserved meatballs.

Chopped fresh mint leaves, to taste (optional)

Chopped fresh cilantro leaves, to taste (optional)

Meatballs

¾ pound extra-lean ground pork

¼ cup minced yellow or white onion

¼ cup minced, drained canned water chestnuts

2 tablespoons coarsely shredded carrot

1 whole green onion, minced

1 tablespoon cooking sherry

1 large egg white

1 teaspoon toasted sesame oil

Divide the pasta among 4 soup bowls. Spoon one-quarter of the reserved soup into each bowl. Top each with 2 tablespoons of the sprouts. Sprinkle with mint and/or cilantro if desired. Serve immediately.

Makes 4 servings

Per serving: 303 calories, 34 g protein, 21 g carbohydrates, 9 g fat (2 g saturated), 60 mg cholesterol, 8 g fiber, 937 mg sodium

MOM'S NEW BEEF STEW

Don't worry, this stew isn't for only moms, but it's sure to taste as good as the one you grew up with. This is a great recipe for a Sunday afternoon while you're home doing the laundry. You'll have a great dinner and plenty of leftovers, which are just as good, if not better.

---

1 tablespoon whole-grain oat flour

⅛ teaspoon garlic power

⅛ teaspoon salt, plus more to taste

Pinch of ground black pepper, plus more to taste

1 pound top round steak, cut into 1" cubes

2 teaspoons extra-virgin olive oil

8 ounces button mushrooms, each halved

1 onion, cut into bite-size pieces

1 tablespoon minced garlic

1 teaspoon dried thyme

2 cans (14 ounces each) lower-sodium, fat-free beef broth

2 large carrots, peeled and cut into bite-size pieces

1 pound sweet potatoes, peeled and cut into 1" cubes

In a medium resealable plastic bag, combine the flour, garlic powder, salt, and pepper. Add the beef and shake the bag until all the cubes are coated. Refrigerate for at least 15 minutes.

Set a large nonstick soup pot over medium-high heat until it is hot enough for a spritz of water to sizzle on it. Add the oil. Add the reserved beef cubes to the pot in a single layer. Cook for about 1 minute per side, or until browned. Reduce the heat to medium. Add the mushrooms, onion, garlic, and thyme. Cook, stirring occasionally with a wooden spoon and scraping any browned bits from the pan bottom, for about 10 minutes, or until the onion is tender.

Add the broth and carrots. Increase the heat to high. When the broth comes to a boil, reduce the heat to low so the mixture simmers gently. Cover and cook for 45 minutes.

Add the potatoes. Cook for 45 minutes, or until the beef is fork tender. Season with additional salt and pepper. Serve immediately.

Makes 4 (2¼-cup) servings

Per serving: 275 calories, 31 g protein, 29 g carbohydrates, 6 g fat (2 g saturated), 50 mg cholesterol, 6 g fiber, 583 mg sodium

Somewhere between 1½ and 2 hours of simmering, the meat will become extremely tender. If it is still tough, simmer it a bit longer.

FUTURE HEARTTHROB'S TURKEY TOMATO SOUP

My friend Stephen mentioned very early in our friendship that when he's bummed, he loves tomato soup. I talked to him one night after he'd just broken up with his girlfriend and he didn't sound so good. I left a care package on his doorstep at lunchtime the next day with a can of tomato soup. Years went by and he mentioned that he was on a diet and that he was in hell eating "cardboard." I developed this muscle-building variety of his ultimate comfort food using all of his favorite herbs. He loved it and I bet you will, too.

1¼ pounds Jennie-O Turkey Store Extra-Lean Ground Turkey

3 tablespoons minced fresh thyme leaves

2½ teaspoons minced fresh sage leaves

½ teaspoon garlic powder

½ teaspoon salt

¼ teaspoon ground black pepper

1½ teaspoons extra-virgin olive oil

2 cups coarsely chopped red onions

1¾ cups coarsely chopped green bell pepper

¾ cup coarsely chopped celery

3 tablespoons minced garlic

1½ cups cooked short-grain brown rice

2 cans (10¾ ounces each) reduced-sodium condensed tomato soup

2 cups water

In a medium bowl, combine the turkey, 1 tablespoon thyme, 1 teaspoon sage, garlic powder, salt, and pepper. With a fork, stir to mix. Set aside.

Set a large nonstick soup pot over medium heat. Add the oil. Place the onions, bell pepper, celery, and garlic in the pot. Cook, stirring occasionally, for 5 to 7 minutes, or until the vegetables start to soften. Push the vegetables to the side of the pot. Increase the heat to medium-high. Place the reserved turkey mixture in the pot. Cook, breaking into chunks with a wooden spoon, for about 8 minutes, or until no longer pink.

Reduce the heat to medium-low. Add the rice, soup, water, the remaining 2 tablespoons thyme, and the remaining 1½ teaspoons sage. Stir to mix. Cook at a simmer, stirring occasionally, for about 15 minutes, or until the flavors are blended. Serve immediately.

Makes 5 (1¾-cup) servings

Per serving: 343 calories, 33 g protein, 44 g carbohydrates, 5 g fat (less than 1 g saturated), 45 mg cholesterol, 4 g fiber, 801 mg sodium

PORK AND BLACK-BEAN VERDE STEW

A twist on traditional Mexican fare, this stew is thick, hearty, and spicy. It's excellent on its own or served over brown rice, which will also turn down the heat if desired. If you can't find no-salt-added black beans, opt for lower-sodium black beans and rinse them well. This stew is a great option to pack for lunch at work on those cold winter days, as it's even better reheated the next day.

2 teaspoons extra-virgin olive oil

1 pound pork loin or tenderloin, trimmed of visible fat and cut into 1" cubes

1¼ cups chopped onions

3 cloves garlic, minced

2 canned chipotle chile peppers in adobo sauce, minced with 1 teaspoon adobo sauce

1 teaspoon dried oregano leaves

¼ teaspoon ground cumin

¼ teaspoon ground coriander

1 bay leaf

1 can (14 ounces) no-salt-added chicken broth

1 can (14½ ounces) no-salt-added diced tomatoes in juice

1 can (14½ ounces) no-salt-added black beans, drained and rinsed

1 cup mild or medium salsa verde

Cooked brown rice (optional)

Place a large nonstick pot over high heat until it is hot enough for a spritz of water to sizzle on it. Add the oil. Heat for 5 to 10 seconds until hot but not smoking. Place the pork in the pot. Cook, stirring occasionally, for 4 to 6 minutes, or until browned on all sides. Add the onions and garlic. Cook, stirring frequently, for 2 to 3 minutes, or until starting to soften. Add the chipotles and sauce, oregano, cumin, coriander, and bay leaf. Stir to mix. Add the broth, tomatoes, beans, and salsa. Stir to mix well. Bring to a boil. Reduce the heat to low.

Cover the pot and simmer for 45 minutes to 1 hour, or until the pork is fork tender. Spoon into bowls over brown rice, if desired. Serve immediately.

Makes 4 (generous 1-cup) servings

Per serving: 308 calories, 33 g protein, 25 g carbohydrates, 7 g fat (2 g saturated), 84 mg cholesterol, 6 g fiber, 414 mg sodium

Any leftovers may be refrigerated in covered plastic storage containers for up to 3 days.

7

Sides and Salads

Salads are nutritious and delicious, but best of all, they're supremely satisfying. Why? Because they take a long time to eat, they're crunchy, and they're filling. You can indulge in a healthy salad with every meal on the Biggest Loser diet—in fact, you should. According to the Biggest Loser diet plan, you should eat a minimum of 4 servings of fruits and vegetables daily. But when we say *minimum,* that means that you can eat more.

Let your creativity run wild when it comes to salads (or just turn to one of the salad recipes in this chapter). It's amazing how much beautiful produce is available at your local supermarket; your neighborhood farmers' market will have even more! There are so many fantastic greens out there that there's just no excuse for a boring salad made from plain old iceberg. For crunch, you can add peppers, cucumber, or celery. For color and flavor, try tomatoes or red onions; for taste and bulk try a blanched green vegetable. And don't forget about sliced mushrooms or bean sprouts—they add lots of volume and texture with hardly any calories.

Even though you'll need to avoid high-fat salad dressings and add-ons, there are other ways to liven up your greens. Try dressing your salads with "good" fats, reduced-fat or fat-free salad dressings, a bit of avocado, or some nuts or seeds. And, of course, you can always add herbs, spices, garlic, lemon or lime juice, and vinegar to your salads with no extra calorie charge!

When it comes to side dishes, round out your main course with something filling. That could mean a vegetable or a whole grain or a combination of the two. When it comes to vegetables, take your pick. Go for grains like brown rice, couscous, grits, whole-wheat pasta, and wild rice. Or pick any one of the fabulous recipes in this chapter. Sides will never be the same again.

PARMESAN-PEPPER SWEET POTATO FRIES

Honestly, I was never really a fan of sweet potatoes . . . until I started eating these fries. My assistant Alex has said the same thing. So if you, too, have been hesitant to jump in and give sweet potatoes another try, it's time you try them with this recipe. You may be surprised that you really do like them after all. If you don't have a good nonstick baking sheet, you can line any baking sheet with parchment paper to make sure the seasonings end up in your mouth instead of on the pan.

½ **pound sweet potatoes, cut into ¼"-thick sticks**

1 **tablespoon grated reduced-fat Parmesan cheese**

½ **teaspoon extra-virgin olive oil**

⅛ **teaspoon garlic powder**

⅛ **teaspoon paprika**

Pinch of cayenne

Salt, to taste

Pinch of ground black pepper

Ketchup (optional)

Preheat the oven to 450°F.

In a medium bowl, toss the potatoes, cheese, olive oil, garlic powder, paprika, cayenne, salt, and black pepper.

Place the potatoes in a single layer on a medium nonstick baking sheet. Bake for 8 minutes. Flip the potatoes and bake for 10 to 12 minutes, or until the potatoes are tender and browned in spots. Serve immediately, with ketchup, if desired.

Makes 1 serving

Per serving: **249 calories, 5 g protein, 49 g carbohydrates, 4 g fat (trace saturated), 8 mg cholesterol, 7 g fiber, 238 mg sodium**

JESSICA LANHAM

Instead of going cold turkey from my favorite things, I have the diet versions and I don't feel like I'm missing a beat.

GARLIC AND CHIVE MASHED SWEET POTATOES

If you've never roasted a head of garlic, it's a great thing to try. One garlic clove has only about 5 calories, a trace of fat, and less than 1 milligram of sodium, so it makes a great seasoning. Roasting garlic tones down its sharp flavor, but also makes it rich and sweet. I love using roasted garlic to season rice dishes and mashed sweet potatoes.

1 head of garlic

¼ teaspoon extra-virgin olive oil

Salt, to taste

Ground black pepper, to taste

2 pounds sweet potatoes, peeled and cut into 1" chunks

3 tablespoons fat-free sour cream

1 tablespoon fat-free milk

4 tablespoons chopped fresh chives

Preheat the oven to 400°F. On a cutting board, slice ¼" off the top end of the garlic bulb to expose the tops of the cloves. Place the bulb, cut side up, on an 8" x 8" piece of aluminum foil. Spoon the oil over the cut side. Season lightly with salt and pepper. Wrap the foil to seal tightly. Bake for about 45 minutes, or until the cloves are tender when pierced with a sharp knife. Let stand for 5 minutes to cool slightly. Squeeze the garlic cloves from their skins into a small bowl. Smash with the back of a spoon. Set aside.

Cook the potatoes in a pot of boiling salted water for 12 to 15 minutes, or until tender when pierced with a fork. Drain and transfer to a medium mixing bowl.

In a small microwaveable bowl, combine the sour cream and milk. Microwave on high power for about 1 minute, or until just warm. Add the milk mixture, the garlic, and 3½ tablespoons of chives to the potatoes. Beat with an electric mixer fitted with beaters until fluffy. Season with salt and pepper. Serve immediately, garnished with the remaining ½ tablespoon chives.

Makes about 5 (½-cup) servings

Per serving: 149 calories, 4 g protein, 33 g carbohydrates, less than 1 g fat (trace saturated), less than 1 mg cholesterol, 5 g fiber, 61 mg sodium

The roasted garlic can be transferred to a small resealable plastic bag or a jar and refrigerated for up to 1 week before using.

DANA'S SPINACH AND FETA BROWN RICE

It took Dana DeSilvio a while to warm up to brown rice. "At first, I thought it was pretty bland," she says, "but Bob told me to try adding things to it to spice it up." Not long thereafter, she found one of her new favorite dishes. She loves the fact that the spinach adds fiber, so it makes her feel fuller.

Photo on page 174

¼ cup chopped sweet onion

1 teaspoon minced garlic

1 cup cooked short-grain brown rice

1 cup chopped fresh spinach leaves

3 tablespoons (about ¾ ounce) crumbled fat-free feta cheese

Salt, to taste

Ground black pepper, to taste

Lightly mist a small, nonstick skillet with olive oil spray. Set over medium heat for 30 seconds. Add the onion and garlic. Cook, stirring occasionally, for 4 to 6 minutes, or until tender. Do not allow to brown. Add the rice and spinach. Cook, stirring constantly, for 3 to 5 minutes, or until the spinach is almost completely wilted. Stir in the cheese. Season with salt and pepper. Serve immediately.

Makes 2 (generous ½-cup) servings

Per serving: 137 calories, 5 g protein, 27 g carbohydrates, less than 1 g fat (trace saturated), 0 mg cholesterol, 3 g fiber, 192 mg sodium

NOT-REALLY-FRIED RICE

If your healthy lifestyle has you missing Chinese takeout, you'll love this dish. It's a bit spicier than traditional fried rice, which is chock full of sodium and fat, but it's considerably healthier and it still gives you that taste of the Orient. I also make this dish with pork tenderloin instead of chicken from time to time so I don't get bored with it.

---

2 teaspoons low-sodium soy sauce

1 teaspoon hot mustard

1 teaspoon chili paste

1 teaspoon toasted sesame oil

3 ounces boneless, skinless chicken breast, trimmed of visible fat and cut into ½" cubes

Salt, to taste

Ground black pepper, to taste

½ cup finely chopped whole green onions

¼ cup chopped carrot

1 clove garlic, minced

¾ cup cooked short-grain brown rice

¼ cup frozen peas

2 large egg whites

In a small bowl, combine the soy sauce, mustard, chili paste, and sesame oil. Stir to mix. Set aside.

Season the chicken with salt and pepper. Set a large, nonstick wok or skillet over medium-high heat until it is hot enough for a spritz of water to sizzle on it. With an oven mitt, briefly remove the pan from the heat to lightly mist with olive oil spray.

Scatter the chicken into the pan. Cook, stirring occasionally, for about 3 minutes, or until browned on all sides and no longer pink inside. Transfer to a plate. Cover to keep warm.

Off the heat, lightly mist the pan with olive oil spray. Set over medium-high heat. Add the green onions, carrot, and garlic to the pan. Cook, stirring frequently, for 2 to 3 minutes. Add the rice and peas. Cook, stirring frequently, for 2 minutes, or until the mixture is hot. Create a well with the rice and veggies to expose the center of the pan. Off the heat, lightly mist the empty part with olive oil spray. Add the egg whites. Stir to mix the egg whites into the rice. Cook for 1 to 2 minutes, or until the egg whites are completely cooked. Return the chicken to the pan. Stir in the reserved soy sauce mixture. Cook, stirring constantly, for about 1 minute, or until hot. Serve immediately.

Makes 1 serving

Per serving: 415 calories, 34 g protein, 50 g carbohydrates, 7 g fat (1 g saturated), 49 mg cholesterol, 7 g fiber, 760 mg sodium

CAJUN "SQUASH YOUR WAISTLINE" FRIES

These spicy fries are a great way to trick your kids (and yourself) into eating squash—even if they think they don't like it! This hearty serving has only 133 calories. Do note that these fries are a bit spicy. If you're not a big fan of spicy food, as my assistants and I are, or you are serving these to your kids, you may want to decrease the amount of cayenne.

Photo on page 168

1 large butternut squash

½ teaspoon extra-virgin olive oil

1 teaspoon paprika

⅛ teaspoon cayenne, or to taste

⅛ teaspoon garlic powder

⅛ teaspoon onion powder

⅛ teaspoon salt

Preheat the oven to 450°F.

Carefully cut both ends off the squash. Using a vegetable peeler, peel the rind from the squash until you've peeled away the pale orange outside layers. Discard the rind. Cut the squash in half lengthwise. With a large spoon, scrape out the seeds and discard them. Cut 8 ounces (about 2 cups) of 4" x ½" sticks. (Refrigerate the remaining squash for another recipe.)

Place the squash sticks in a medium mixing bowl. Add the oil, paprika, cayenne, garlic powder, onion powder, and salt. Toss to coat. Transfer the squash to a baking sheet so the sticks are in a single layer and do not touch.

Bake, turning the squash about every 5 minutes, for 22 for 25 minutes, or until the outsides are crisp and the insides are tender when tested with a fork. Serve immediately.

Makes 1 serving

Per serving: 133 calories, 3 g protein, 28 g carbohydrates, 3 g fat (trace saturated), 0 mg cholesterol, 5 g fiber, 302 mg sodium

MELINDA'S HOLIDAY SPINACH

Melinda Suttle quickly found this dish after arriving at the ranch. She's excited about making it for her husband. "The green of the spinach and the red of the pepper give the dish a festive appearance," she says. "It's wonderful to serve for holidays, but equally yummy for any occasion." Melinda substitutes ¹/₂ cup of low-fat plain soy milk for the cream cheese and adds a couple of table-spoons of olive oil. I prefer the creaminess of the version below.

1 teaspoon extra-virgin olive oil

¹/₂ cup chopped white onion

²/₃ cup chopped red bell pepper

¹/₃ cup sliced fresh mushrooms

1 clove garlic, minced

1 bag (9 ounces) baby spinach leaves (12 cups), coarsely chopped

3 tablespoons light cream cheese from a block, at room temperature

Set a large nonstick skillet over medium heat. Add the olive oil. Heat for 30 seconds. Add the onion. Cook, stirring occasionally, for 2 minutes. Add the bell pepper, mushrooms, and garlic. Cook, stirring occasionally, for 5 to 7 minutes, or until the vegetables are tender. Add the spinach. Cook, stirring constantly, for 2 to 3 minutes, or until the leaves are wilted. Remove from the heat. Add the cream cheese. Stir until the cheese melts. Serve immediately.

Makes 3 (²/₃-cup) servings

Per serving: **91 calories, 5 g protein, 9 g carbohydrates, 5 g fat (2 g saturated), 13 mg cholesterol, 3 g fiber, 139 mg sodium**

PARMESAN-ROASTED CAULIFLOWER

Among my friends who like cauliflower, this is a huge favorite. In fact every person who tries it looks surprised that they enjoy it as much as they do. If you've ever enjoyed a cauliflower dish, I suggest you add this to your "must-try" list.

1½ cups (6 ounces) cauliflower florets

2 teaspoons grated reduced-fat Parmesan cheese

1 teaspoon chopped fresh parsley leaves

¼ teaspoon garlic powder

¼ teaspoon ground black pepper

Salt, to taste

1 teaspoon extra-virgin olive oil

Preheat the oven to 425°F.

In a medium bowl, combine the cauliflower, cheese, parsley, garlic powder, and pepper. Season with salt. Toss to mix. Drizzle on the oil and toss again. Transfer the mixture to a small nonstick baking dish.

Bake for 15 to 17 minutes, tossing once, or until lightly browned and crisp-tender. Serve immediately.

Makes 1 serving

Per serving: **104 calories, 4 g protein, 11 g carbohydrates, 6 g fat (less than 1 g saturated), 5 mg cholesterol, 4 g fiber, 121 mg sodium**

MATT HOOVER

When you first start a diet, get a garbage bag and empty out your refrigerator and pantry, then restock them with healthy food.

BRUSCHETTA EGGPLANT

Now that I try not to overdo it on the carbs, I like to find ways to morph my favorite bread toppings into healthier dishes. Here I've taken the principle ingredients in traditional bruschetta and used them to season eggplant. For an even different twist, try skipping the eggplant and add the mixture to brown rice, barley, or another healthy grain.

1 pound eggplant, unpeeled, cut into 1" cubes

Pinch of garlic powder, or to taste

3 medium plum tomatoes, seeded and chopped

1 whole green onion, chopped

1 clove garlic, minced

2 tablespoons chopped fresh basil leaves

Salt, to taste

Ground black pepper, to taste

Preheat the oven to 400°F.

Lightly mist a medium, nonstick baking sheet with olive oil spray. Place the eggplant in a single layer on the baking sheet so the cubes do not touch. Lightly mist the eggplant with olive oil spray. Sprinkle on the garlic powder.

Bake for 7 to 10 minutes. Flip and bake for 7 to 10 minutes more, or until tender when tested with a fork.

In a large serving bowl, combine the tomatoes, green onion, garlic, and basil. Add the eggplant. Season with salt and pepper. Toss gently to mix. Serve immediately.

Makes 2 servings

Per serving: 79 calories, 3 g protein, 18 g carbohydrates, 1 g fat (trace saturated), 0 mg cholesterol, 9 g fiber, 11 mg sodium

ANDREA'S BALSAMIC-ROASTED ASPARAGUS

Andrea Overstreet juggles a busy life of being a hairdresser, wife, and mom, so she doesn't have a lot of time to cook. By keeping recipes simple and doing a little prep work in advance, she takes the guesswork out of dinner. Andrea loves to cook and make up new recipes. This one is a favorite veggie dish that takes only minutes to prepare.

4 medium asparagus spears, ends trimmed, cut into 3" lengths

½ red bell pepper, cut into ½"-wide strips

1 tablespoon balsamic vinegar

1 teaspoon extra-virgin olive oil

Salt, to taste

Ground black pepper, to taste

Preheat the oven to 400°F.

In a large, resealable plastic bag, combine the asparagus, red pepper, vinegar, and oil. Shake the bag to coat well. Place the asparagus and red pepper on a small nonstick baking sheet. Season with salt and pepper. Spread the pieces out so they are not touching.

Bake for 15 minutes, or until crisp-tender and lightly browned. Serve immediately.

Makes 1 serving

Per serving: 89 calories, 3 g protein, 10 g carbohydrates, 5 g fat (less than 1 g saturated), 0 mg cholesterol, 3 g fiber, 8 mg sodium

BOBBY'S BROCCOLI WITH CHEESE SAUCE

Bobby Moore is the cook in his firehouse. "I can't go back there and serve plain steamed broccoli and expect the guys eat it," he says. "Though none of us would mind eating healthier, the guys aren't exactly going to eat rabbit food." While at the ranch, he has been conjuring up all sorts of dishes and trying them out on other contestants. This one has been a hit; it tastes good and it helps everyone fill up on veggies without excess fat and calories.

3 cups (½ pound) broccoli florets

¼ cup Tostitos Reduced Fat Zesty Cheese Dip

In a medium saucepan, bring 4 cups of water to a boil over high heat. Add the broccoli. Cook for about 3 minutes, or until crisp-tender. Drain and pat dry. Divide between 2 serving plates.

Meanwhile, spoon the dip into a small microwaveable bowl. Microwave on low power in 10-second intervals, until just warm. Spoon half of the dip evenly over each portion of broccoli. Serve immediately.

Makes 2 servings

Per serving: 72 calories, 4 g protein, 10 g carbohydrates, 2 g fat (1 g saturated), 4 mg cholesterol, 4 g fiber, 241 mg sodium

TRAINER TIP: **KIM LYONS**

Natural, unprocessed foods are used more efficiently by the body and are less likely to be stored as body fat. Choose fresh fruits, veggies, whole grains, and other complex carbs as the mainstays of your diet.

HAZELNUT AND LEMON GREEN BEANS

Very early in my catering career, I was hired by a well-known producer to cater his family's Thanksgiving dinner. They wanted a traditional dinner as well as a vegan alternative and were having trouble finding someone willing to do it. Since they offered me 300 dollars per person, I was up for creating anything they wanted. I was told that the lady of the house loved green beans and lemons. This was the resulting veggie dish . . . and I still can't look at it without seeing dollar signs.

Photo on page 178

½   pound green beans, ends trimmed

¼   teaspoon salt, plus more to taste

2   teaspoons coarsely chopped hazelnuts, toasted

1½   teaspoons grated lemon peel

2   teaspoons lemon juice, preferably fresh-squeezed

½   teaspoon extra-virgin olive oil

    Ground black pepper, to taste

Fill a large pot one-third full of water. Cover and set over high heat. When the water comes to a full boil, add the beans and ¼ teaspoon salt. Cook for 4 to 6 minutes, or until just tender. Drain in a colander. Transfer to a serving bowl. Add the nuts, peel, juice, and oil. Season with salt and pepper. Toss gently to mix. Serve immediately.

Makes 2 servings

Per serving: 55 calories, 2 g protein, 8 g carbohydrates, 3 g fat (trace saturated), 0 mg cholesterol, 5 g fiber, 14 mg sodium

To toast the hazelnuts, place them in a dry, nonstick skillet over high heat. Cook for 1 to 3 minutes, shaking every 15 seconds or so, until toasted. Watch them closely, as they brown quickly.

MO'S SPINACH-RICOTTA BAKE

Raised on Southern favorites like fried chicken and banana pudding, Mo Walker has made a valiant effort to add veggies galore to his daily diet. He's actually starting to look forward to them. "I love this spinach dish," he says, "it reminds me of stuffed shell filling." I agree—and I like it because it has plenty of filling fiber, yet it seems more like an Italian favorite than a veggie dish.

1 package (1 pound) frozen chopped spinach, thawed

1 container (15 ounces) fat-free ricotta cheese

3 tablespoons grated reduced-fat Parmesan cheese

2 large egg whites

¼ teaspoon garlic powder

Pinch of ground nutmeg

1½ cups Superior Spaghetti Sauce (page 191), or other low-sodium, low-fat marinara sauce

Preheat the oven to 400°F. Lightly mist an 8" x 8" baking dish with olive oil spray.

Place the spinach in the center of a clean dishtowel. Fold the towel over the spinach and squeeze out as much moisture as possible. (This is important so the dish won't be watery.) Place in a large mixing bowl. Add the ricotta, Parmesan, egg whites, garlic powder, and nutmeg. Stir to mix. Transfer to the prepared dish. With the back of a spoon, spread it out to fill the dish. Bake for 20 minutes, or until it is hot through and the top is starting to brown. Let stand for 5 minutes to cool slightly.

Place the sauce in a microwaveable bowl. Microwave on low power in 15-second intervals until warm. Cut the spinach-ricotta bake into 6 equal pieces. Transfer each piece to a serving plate. Spoon ¼ cup of sauce over each serving. Serve immediately. Store the leftovers in a resealable plastic container for up to 3 days.

Makes 6 servings

Per serving: **134 calories, 11 g protein, 17 g carbohydrates, 2 g fat (trace saturated), 15 mg cholesterol, 3 g fiber, 304 mg sodium**

STRENGTH-BUILDERS' STUFFED MUSHROOMS

I generally prefer reduced-fat to fat-free feta cheese, but these mushrooms are surprisingly tasty with fat-free. Though the directions say to use ⅛ teaspoon cayenne, I'd recommend that you use somewhere between a pinch and ⅛ teaspoon. A pinch seems too little and ⅛ teaspoon seems slightly too much. That said, if you love mushrooms, you just may find these to be a regular part of your repertoire after the first bite.

4   medium button mushrooms

1½   tablespoons crumbled fat-free feta cheese (⅓ ounce)

2   teaspoons chopped fresh flat-leaf parsley

½   teaspoon extra-virgin olive oil

⅛   teaspoon cayenne, or to taste

Preheat the oven to 425°F. Lightly mist a small baking dish with olive oil spray.

Remove the stems from the mushrooms by gently twisting the stem until it comes loose and pulls from the mushroom top. Mince the stems and place in a small mixing bowl. Place the caps in the prepared baking dish stemmed-side up.

Add the cheese, parsley, oil, and cayenne to the bowl. Stir to mix well. Spoon the mixture evenly into the reserved mushroom caps. Divide the remaining mixture evenly among the caps, mounding the filling on each.

Bake for 12 to 15 minutes, or until tender. Let the mushrooms stand to cool slightly before serving.

Makes 1 serving

Per serving: 48 calories, 4 g protein, 3 g carbohydrates, 3 g fat (trace saturated), 0 mg cholesterol, less than 1 g fiber, 157 mg sodium

LIZZETH'S CUCUMBER SALAD

Lizzeth Davalos has always loved fatty foods, but she also admits that they seemed more convenient. "When I'd come home from a long day, I'd just grab the first thing I could find," she says, "which was often a cookie or other junk food." When she returned from the ranch, she started making sure her refrigerator was packed with celery and carrot sticks and chunks of lean meats. But she also loves this spin on traditional cucumber salad, which she can make and then store in the refrigerator for 5 days, so it's there when she's hungry.

3 medium cucumbers, unpeeled, sliced paper-thin

½ medium red or white onion, finely slivered

3 cups cold water

1½ cups white vinegar

3 packets (.035 ounce each) sugar substitute (such as Splenda)

½ teaspoon salt

½ teaspoon ground black pepper

In a plastic storage container, combine the cucumbers, onion, water, vinegar, sugar substitute, salt, and pepper. Stir to mix. Cover the container with a lid. Refrigerate for at least a few hours or as long as 5 days. Serve cold.

Makes 6 (1¼-cup) servings

Per serving: **40 calories, 2 g protein, 6 g carbohydrates, 0 g fat, 0 mg cholesterol, 2 g fiber, 195 mg sodium**

FRESH AND COLORFUL JICAMA SLAW

If you've never used jicama, ask the produce guy (or gal) at your local grocery store or farmers' market to point it out. It's way more common than you might imagine and extremely low in calories. I think it tastes like a cross between an apple and a water chestnut. It's a perfect fit for this crunchy, fresh, and flavorful salad that is sure to be a hit at a summer barbecue or as a side dish anytime. If you have a food processor with a julienne blade, it's easy to make this salad in minutes.

1 English cucumber, seeded and cut into thin 1"-long strips

½ pound jicama, peeled and cut into thin 1"-long strips

2 medium carrots, peeled and cut into thin 1"-long strips

6 tablespoons chopped fresh cilantro leaves

5 tablespoons lime juice, preferably fresh-squeezed

1 tablespoon extra-virgin olive oil

1½ teaspoons red-pepper flakes

Salt, to taste

Ground black pepper, to taste

In a mixing bowl, combine the cucumber, jicama, carrots, cilantro, lime juice, oil, and pepper flakes. Season with salt and pepper. Toss gently to mix. Serve immediately or refrigerate for up to 3 days.

Makes 4 servings

Per serving: 80 calories, 2 g protein, 11 g carbohydrates, 4 g fat (less than 1 g saturated), 0 mg cholesterol, 2 g fiber, 25 mg sodium

BROCCOLI SALAD WITH SWEET VINAIGRETTE

If you can coordinate making this salad a day in advance, it's well worth trying to do so. Though it's good immediately, by the next day, the flavors meld so nicely, you're likely to swear that this is as special as any full-fat broccoli salad.

3 tablespoons orange juice, preferably fresh-squeezed

2 tablespoons fat-free plain yogurt

2 teaspoons stone ground mustard

1 teaspoon 100% fruit orange marmalade preserves

1½ cups (3½ ounces) broccoli florets, coarsely chopped

2 tablespoons chopped red onion

In a plastic storage container, whisk together the juice, yogurt, mustard, and preserves. Add the broccoli and onion. Toss to coat. Cover the container with the lid. Refrigerate for at least 1 hour or up to 1 day before serving.

Makes 1 serving

Per serving: 85 calories, 5 g protein, 18 g carbohydrates, less than 1 g fat (trace saturated), less than 1 mg cholesterol, 3 g fiber, 177 mg sodium

THAI GROUND-CHICKEN SALAD

If you've ever enjoyed a larb salad at a Thai restaurant, this salad may have a familiar taste. I love the freshness of the lime juice, which is the base of the dressing. Make sure you buy dry-roasted cashews. If the package doesn't say, flip it over and look at the label. If the nuts have been dry-roasted, you won't see any oils included in the ingredient list. I think all nuts are yummier when not roasted in oil—and they're definitely better for you.

2 tablespoons lime juice, preferably fresh squeezed

2 teaspoons minced fresh ginger

1 teaspoon honey

⅛ teaspoon chili garlic sauce, or to taste

⅛ teaspoon salt

1½ teaspoons extra-virgin olive oil

¼ pound extra-lean ground chicken

2 cups shredded romaine lettuce leaves

½ cup shredded carrot

¼ cup red onion slivers

2 tablespoons chopped fresh mint leaves

1 tablespoon chopped fresh cilantro leaves

1 to 2 tablespoons chopped dry-roasted cashews

In a small bowl, combine the lime juice, ginger, honey, chili garlic sauce, and salt. Whisk, gradually adding the oil, until blended.

Set a small nonstick frying pan over medium-high heat until it is hot enough for a spritz of water to sizzle on it. With an oven mitt, briefly remove the pan from the heat to lightly mist with olive oil spray. Add the chicken to the pan. Cook, breaking up the meat into chunks with a spatula, for 3 to 5 minutes, or until no longer pink. Remove from the heat. Stir in 1 tablespoon of the reserved dressing.

In a large serving bowl, combine the lettuce, carrot, onion, mint, and cilantro. Drizzle with the remaining dressing and toss. Top with the reserved chicken and sprinkle with the nuts. Serve immediately.

Makes 1 serving

Per serving: 333 calories, 30 g protein, 25 g carbohydrates, 13 g fat (2 g saturated), 66 mg cholesterol, 5 g fiber, 482 mg sodium

DELI CHOPPED SALAD

The key to restaurant-quality chopped salad is to make sure all the veggies are washed and then dried well—there's nothing worse than a soggy salad. Also, by chopping the ingredients finely, the flavors mix, so you don't need to use exorbitant amounts of dressing to get a flavor explosion with every bite. If you don't plan on enjoying this main-dish salad immediately, don't add the dressing until just before serving. And be sure to remove the seeds from the tomato, which can also make your salad soggy over time.

3 cups finely chopped romaine lettuce leaves

½ cup (2 ounces) diced BBQ Turkey Breast Roast (page 175) or other lean, low-sodium deli-style turkey

⅓ cup (1½ ounces) diced Rosemary-Grilled London Broil (page 159) or other lean, low-sodium deli-style roast beef

⅓ cup (1½ ounces) diced low-fat mozzarella cheese

½ cup finely chopped, seeded tomato

¼ cup loosely packed fresh basil leaves, finely chopped

3 tablespoons finely chopped red onion

2 tablespoons low-fat Italian salad dressing

Red-pepper flakes, to taste (optional)

In a large serving bowl, combine the lettuce, turkey, beef, cheese, tomato, basil, onion, and dressing. Toss to coat the ingredients with the dressing. Season with pepper flakes, if desired. Serve immediately.

Makes 1 serving

Per serving: 289 calories, 36 g protein, 18 g carbohydrates, 10 g fat (3 g saturated), 53 mg cholesterol, 7 g fiber, 632 mg sodium

GREEK GOD(DESS) SALAD

Extremely light and lemony, this is one of my all-time favorite recipes for eating lots of veggies. I've served this to dinner guests many times and they often ask what is in the dressing. When they find out that the only fat comes from a few olives and an ounce of reduced-fat feta, they're always surprised. This recipe makes two side-dish servings or, with the grilled chicken, one main-dish serving. I tend to splurge and use reduced-fat rather than fat-free feta, but when I'm trying to maximize my weight loss and not just maintaining, I sometimes do opt for the fat-free. Whatever you do, though, please don't substitute dried parsley or bottled lemon juice—if you do, it's on you.

3 tablespoons minced fresh parsley leaves

4 pitted kalamata olives, minced

1 clove garlic, minced

4 to 5 tablespoons lemon juice (preferably fresh squeezed), to taste

½ medium cucumber, seeded and chopped

½ medium red or orange bell pepper, chopped

1 medium tomato, seeded and chopped

⅓ cup finely chopped red onion

1 ounce (heaping ¼ cup) crumbled reduced-fat feta cheese

1 small (4-ounce) grilled chicken breast, sliced (optional)

In a serving bowl, combine the parsley, olives, and garlic. Whisk in 4 tablespoons lemon juice. Add the cucumber, bell pepper, tomato, onion, and 3 tablespoons of the cheese. Toss to coat the ingredients with the dressing. Taste and add up to 1 tablespoon more lemon juice, if desired. Scatter the chicken over the salad, if desired. Top with the remaining cheese.

Makes 2 servings

Per serving: 106 calories, 5 g protein, 15 g carbohydrates, 4 g fat (1 g saturated), 5 mg cholesterol, 3 g fiber, 315 mg sodium

You can use fat-free feta, which will eliminate 3 grams of fat. However, I much prefer the flavor of the reduced-fat feta which also tends to have less carbohydrates and less sodium than fat-free. In addition, reduced-fat tends to be easier to find.

TRUDI'S CHICKEN SALAD À LA SUZY

Online club member Trudi Frazel writes, "This is the salad I take to work every day for lunch. Simple to prepare, this is a hearty, tasty meal that I actually look forward to!" Making salads in resealable plastic bags was inspired by a tip posted by Suzy Preston on the Biggest Loser Club Web site (www.biggestloserclub.com). Trudi adds, "In the roughly six weeks I have been using this meal (instead of eating at work), I have lost 10 pounds."

1 pound boneless, skinless chicken breasts, trimmed of visible fat

2 tablespoons Worcestershire sauce

1 tablespoon hot-pepper sauce

1 tablespoon lemon juice, preferably fresh squeezed

10 cups (about 10 ounces) spring mix salad greens

1 bell pepper (any color), sliced into strips

1 large cucumber, seeded and cut into bite-sized chunks

32 baby carrots

1 cup alfalfa, broccoli, or mung bean sprouts

4 to 8 tablespoons light balsamic vinaigrette

In a large, resealable plastic bag, combine the chicken, Worcestershire sauce, hot-pepper sauce, and lemon juice. Seal the bag. Shake until the chicken is coated. Refrigerate for 1 to 2 hours for the seasonings to flavor the chicken.

Preheat a grill to high heat. Remove the chicken from the bag. Discard the marinade bag. Lightly mist the chicken with olive oil spray. Place the chicken on the grill. Reduce the heat to low. (If it is not possible to reduce the heat, sear the chicken quickly on both sides and then move away from direct heat.) Cook for 3 to 5 minutes per side, or until the chicken is no longer pink and the juices run clear. Transfer the chicken to a plate. Let stand for 10 minutes. Cover with plastic wrap. Refrigerate for at least 30 minutes or up to 3 days.

To prepare the salad: Cut the cooled chicken breasts into bite-sized strips. Among 4 large, resealable plastic bags, evenly divide the salad greens, bell pepper, cucumber, carrots, sprouts, and the reserved chicken. Seal the bags. Refrigerate for up to 3 days. Before packing for lunch, add 1 to 2 tablespoons of the vinaigrette to a bag and seal.

Just before serving, shake the bag to toss the salad with the vinaigrette. Pour into a serving bowl or eat from the bag.

Makes 4 servings

Per serving: **258 calories, 32 g protein, 24 g carbohydrates, 4 g fat (less than 1 g saturated), 66 mg cholesterol, 8 g fiber, 463 mg sodium**

RED, GREEN, AND BLUE SALAD

One of my ex-boyfriends always wanted to cook for me. Though I truly appreciated the gesture, I always dreaded it. He'd inevitably spend an entire day cooking—making it impossible for us to spend time together—then I'd have to sit there as he'd boast about his rubbery steaks. (How did he not understand that they were rubbery?) However, he once pulled off a more fattening version of this salad, which caught my attention. I never fell in love with him, but I came close to falling in love with this simple salad with only 63 calories.

2 medium plum tomatoes, seeded and chopped

½ medium cucumber, seeded and chopped

¼ cup red onion slivers

2 tablespoons crumbled gorgonzola cheese

2 teaspoons light balsamic salad dressing

Salt, to taste

Ground black pepper, to taste

In a medium serving bowl, combine the tomatoes, cucumber, onion, cheese, and dressing. Toss well. Season with salt and pepper. Serve immediately.

Makes 2 (1½-cup) servings

Per serving: 63 calories, 3 g protein, 7 g carbohydrates, 3 g fat (2 g saturated), 6 mg cholesterol, 2 g fiber, 177 mg sodium

HOT AND COLD BROWN-RICE SALAD

This is a great dish to take to work for lunch. Just pack the rice separately and heat it in the microwave before mixing it into the chicken-veggie mixture—the key is making sure the rice is piping hot before you add it to the cold ingredients. The hot-cold combo is what makes it unique and especially tasty. If you think you don't like brown rice, try short-grain before you make a final decision. I much prefer it to medium- or long-grain.

¾ cup (4 ounces) grilled chicken, chilled and chopped

⅓ cup finely chopped broccoli florets

⅓ cup chopped red bell pepper

2 tablespoons chopped red onion

1 tablespoon light Italian salad dressing

1 tablespoon balsamic vinegar, or to taste

¾ cup cooked short-grain brown rice

Salt, to taste

Ground black pepper, to taste

In a medium bowl, combine the chicken, broccoli, red pepper, onion, dressing, and 1 tablespoon vinegar. Toss to coat the ingredients with the dressing and set aside.

If the rice isn't hot, place it in a small microwaveable bowl. Microwave on low power in 15-second intervals until hot.

Add the rice to the chicken mixture, and season with salt, pepper, and 1 tablespoon vinegar, if desired. Serve immediately.

Makes 1 serving

Per serving: **368 calories, 34 g protein, 44 g carbohydrates, 5 g fat (less than 1 g saturated), 74 mg cholesterol, 5 g fiber, 211 mg sodium**

BOBBY MOORE

When eating out, ask for a to-go box as soon as you receive your meal. Immediately put half of your meal in the box and save it for later.

8

Main Courses

After a long day on the job, at school, or taking care of the kids, it's hard to find the time or energy to whip up dinner—especially one that's healthy and well-balanced. It's no wonder that so many of us drive through the local fast food joint, pick up prepared food from the neighborhood market, call up for pizza or Chinese food, or pop something frozen in the microwave. When you're exhausted and in a hurry, it's natural to want to take the path of least resistance.

But as hard as it is to believe, there really is an alternative—like the recipes in this chapter. Many are quick and easy, and they're all healthy and guaranteed to please the entire family—including children. Who wouldn't love dishes like Rosemary-Grilled London Broil or Amanda's Cheesy Eggplant Lasagna?

Cooking requires a little bit of advance planning, but you'll find that taking a bit of time to organize and shop will pay off—in dollars saved and pounds lost! Try doing prep work in the morning before you leave the house so that you can hit the ground running when you get home.

Nothing satisfies like a home-cooked meal that requires minimum effort. Wouldn't you love to come home to something like Mustard and Herb-Baked Salmon?

SPICY MEATBALLS WITH FIERY CHILI SAUCE

One of the most frustrating obstacles at mealtime in the days I was desperately trying to lose weight was thinking I couldn't eat meatballs. I love love love them! A twist on this recipe was one of the first healthier varieties I'd eaten and I was instantly hooked. Now, I enjoy lean meatballs galore and this recipe happens to be one of my favorites! Though it's made with beef (I also love it with lean ground veal), it's even leaner than the chicken and turkey ones I've seen in grocery and even health food stores.

¼ pound 96% lean ground beef

2 tablespoons cooked brown rice

¼ teaspoon dried parsley

¼ teaspoon Italian seasoning

¼ teaspoon fennel seeds

⅛ teaspoon garlic powder

⅛ teaspoon red-pepper flakes

⅛ teaspoon dried minced onion

Pinch of salt

Pinch of black pepper

2½ tablespoons chili sauce

⅛ teaspoon hot-pepper sauce, or more to taste

Preheat the oven to 400°F.

In a medium bowl, combine the beef, rice, parsley, Italian seasoning, fennel, garlic powder, red-pepper flakes, onion, salt, and pepper. With clean hands or a fork, mix well. With a 1" cookie scoop or a spoon and your hands, form the mixture into eight 1" meatballs. Place the meatballs in a single layer on a small nonstick baking sheet. Bake for about 7 minutes, or until the meatballs are just barely pink inside. Transfer to a medium bowl and set aside.

Meanwhile, in a small bowl, combine the chili sauce with the hot-pepper sauce. Pour the sauce over the meatballs. Toss to coat with sauce. Serve immediately.

Makes 1 serving

Per serving: 206 calories, 23 g protein, 17 g carbohydrates, 5 g fat (2 g saturated), 60 mg cholesterol, less than 1 g fiber, 678 mg sodium

NEW-FASHIONED MEAT LOAF

Though it's very low in fat, this is one of my all-time favorite meat loaves. The tanginess of the horse-radish coupled with the ketchup makes it unique. Made with veal or beef, it's extremely moist, even compared to full-fat meat loaf. Though I don't like many low-carb ketchups, I use Heinz One Carb Ketchup here, which many of my testers claimed to enjoy even more than traditional ketchup.

⅔ cup old-fashioned oats

½ cup fat-free milk

1 pound 97% lean ground veal or 96% lean ground beef

½ cup chopped fresh spinach leaves

¼ cup minced onion

2 large egg whites, lightly beaten

1 tablespoon prepared horseradish

2 teaspoons Italian seasoning

1 teaspoon Worcestershire sauce

1 clove garlic, minced

½ teaspoon salt

⅓ cup reduced-sugar or unsweetened ketchup (such as Heinz One Carb)

Preheat the oven to 350°F. Lightly mist an 8½" x 4¼" x 3" nonstick loaf pan with olive oil spray. Set aside.

In a medium mixing bowl, combine the oats and the milk. Let stand for 3 minutes, or until the oats are slightly softened. Add the veal or beef, spinach, onion, egg whites, horseradish, Italian seasoning, Worcestershire sauce, garlic, and salt. With clean hands or a fork, mix well. Transfer the mixture to the prepared pan. Press into the pan, patting the top flat. Spread the ketchup over the top.

Bake for 30 minutes, or until a thermometer inserted in the center registers 160°F and the meat is no longer pink. Let sit for 10 minutes. Cut into 8 slices. Serve immediately.

Makes 4 (2-slice) servings

Per serving: 224 calories, 29 g protein, 14 g carbohydrates, 5 g fat (1 g saturated), 91 mg cholesterol, 2 g fiber, 552 mg sodium

For a firmer meat loaf, use only one egg white. Two will make it extra moist—so much that it almost crumbles.

ROSEMARY-GRILLED LONDON BROIL

This roast is so simple, it only takes about 15 minutes from start to finish. You'll have a delicious dinner and leftovers that are a great alternative to deli meats that are often full of sodium and fillers. Just be sure to slice it extremely thin (almost shaved) by hand on a meat slicer for sandwiches or cut it into small cubes (½ inch is great) to throw into salads. Bigger pieces or thicker slices might seem tough after it's been chilled.

1	tablespoon minced garlic
1½	teaspoons dried rosemary
½	teaspoon extra-virgin olive oil
¼	teaspoon salt
¼	teaspoon ground black pepper
2	pounds beef London broil, trimmed of visible fat

Preheat the grill to high heat.

In a small dish, combine the garlic, rosemary, oil, salt, and pepper. Rub the garlic mixture evenly over the roast. Let the beef stand 5 minutes.

Grill the beef for 5 to 6 minutes per side, or until desired doneness. (A thermometer inserted in the center registers 145°F for medium-rare/160°F for medium/165°F for well done.) Tent it with foil and let stand for 10 minutes. Cut into thin slices against the grain of the meat. Serve immediately.

Makes 6 (4-ounce) servings

Per serving: **175 calories, 33 g protein, 5 g carbohydrates, 5 g fat (2 g saturated), 67 mg cholesterol, trace fiber, 173 mg sodium**

SUZY PRESTON

When dining out, be picky. Literally! Pick off all the things that you know aren't good for you. Better yet, have the chef leave them off to begin with.

SWEET-AND-SPICY PORK TENDERLOIN

When people hear that I'm a "healthy chef," they often assume I'm a vegetarian, which, to anyone who knows me, is a ridiculous notion. I love meat . . . all kinds really, but this pork roast is of my favorites. In fact, my friend Marjorie and I made this roast one night and we loved it so much we wanted to eat the whole thing. When cooked right, this is as tender as can be.

½ teaspoon ground cumin

½ teaspoon ground cinnamon

½ teaspoon salt

¼ teaspoon ground black pepper

¼ teaspoon ground allspice

⅛ teaspoon garlic powder

⅛ teaspoon ground chipotle chile pepper

1 pork tenderloin (1¼ pounds), trimmed of visible fat

1 teaspoon extra-virgin olive oil

2 tablespoons honey

1 tablespoon minced garlic

1½ teaspoons hot-pepper sauce

Preheat the oven to 350°F. Lightly mist a small roasting pan or oven-proof skillet with olive oil spray. Set aside.

In a small bowl, combine the cumin, cinnamon, salt, black pepper, allspice, garlic powder, and chipotle pepper. Rub the pork evenly with the olive oil. Then rub evenly with the spice mixture until coated. Cover loosely with plastic wrap. Refrigerate for 15 minutes.

Meanwhile, in a small bowl, combine the honey, garlic, and hot-pepper sauce. Whisk to mix. Set aside.

Set a large nonstick skillet over medium-high heat until it is hot enough for a spritz of water to sizzle on it. With an oven mitt, briefly remove the pan from the heat to lightly mist with olive oil spray. Place the pork in the pan. Cook for 1 minute per side, or until browned on all sides. Transfer to the prepared pan. With a basting brush, evenly coat the pork with the reserved honey mixture.

Roast the tenderloin in the oven for 16 to 18 minutes, or until a thermometer inserted in the center reaches 160°F and the juices run clear. Remove from the oven. Cover the pork loosely with aluminum foil. Let stand for 10 minutes. Transfer the pork to a cutting board. Holding a knife at a 45° angle, cut into thin slices. Serve immediately.

Makes 4 servings

Per serving: 221 calories, 30 g protein, 10 g carbohydrates, 6 g fat (2 g saturated), 92 mg cholesterol, less than 1 g fiber, 375 mg sodium

DARI'S PICANTE CHICKEN

Navy wife Dari O'Brien loves to play in the kitchen with all of her knowledge from the ranch. "Not everything always works the way I plan when I'm in the kitchen, but I have found a few meals that I love and so does my family," she says. The most important thing to her is that she stick to a low-calorie and low-carb way of cooking. This recipe is both.

⅓ cup plus ½ cup mild, medium, or hot picante sauce

4 medium (4-ounce) boneless, skinless chicken breasts, trimmed of visible fat

6 tablespoons light cream cheese from a block, softened

½ cup (1 ounce) finely shredded Cabot 75% Light Cheddar Cheese

Preheat the oven to 350°F. Spread ⅓ cup of the picante sauce in the bottom of a 13" x 9" baking dish. Set aside.

Lay chicken breasts on a cutting board. Use the flat side of a meat mallet to pound the chicken breasts to a uniform thickness.

Spread the chicken evenly with the cream cheese. Lay the chicken, cream cheese up, in a single layer in the prepared baking dish. Spoon the remaining ½ cup picante sauce evenly over the breasts. Cover the dish with aluminum foil.

Bake for 15 minutes. Remove the aluminum foil. Sprinkle the Cheddar cheese evenly over the breasts. Bake, uncovered, for 15 minutes, or until no longer pink. Serve immediately.

Makes 4 servings

Per serving: 198 calories, 30 g protein, 4 g carbohydrates, 6 g fat (3 g saturated), 83 mg cholesterol, 1 g fiber, 591 mg sodium

COMPETITOR'S CHICKEN CURRY

If you thought your healthy lifestyle meant that you had to avoid Indian food, this dish will change your mind. And it is likely to become a favorite, as it has become one of mine. I love to serve the curry over brown rice and I often accompany it with a cucumber salad or a cucumber and tomato salad.

¾ pound boneless, skinless chicken breasts, trimmed of visible fat and cut into 1" cubes

Salt, to taste

Ground black pepper, to taste

2 teaspoons extra-virgin olive oil

¼ cup chopped white or yellow onion

¼ cup chopped celery

2 cloves garlic, minced

2 tablespoons whole-grain oat flour

1 cup low-sodium chicken broth

½ cup canned no-salt-added diced tomatoes in juice

½ teaspoon Worcestershire sauce

½ to 1 teaspoon curry powder, to taste

⅛ teaspoon cayenne

¼ cup chopped fresh cilantro leaves

Season the chicken with salt and black pepper.

Set a medium nonstick skillet over medium-high heat until a spritz of water sizzles on it. Add 1 teaspoon of oil to the pan. Scatter the chicken pieces in the pan. Cook, stirring frequently, for 3 to 5 minutes, or until the chicken cubes are browned. Cook, lowering the heat slightly if needed, for 2 to 4 minutes, or until the chicken is no longer pink. Transfer the chicken to a plate. Set aside.

Reduce the heat to medium. Add the remaining 1 teaspoon of oil to pan. Add the onion, celery, and garlic. Cook, stirring occasionally, for about 5 minutes, or until just starting to brown. Stir in the flour until well combined. Add the broth. Cook, stirring constantly, for 4 to 5 minutes, or until thickened. Stir in the tomatoes, Worcestershire sauce, ½ teaspoon curry powder, cayenne, and the reserved chicken. Simmer for 2 to 3 minutes for the flavors to blend. Taste and add up to ½ teaspoon more curry powder, if desired. Turn off the heat and stir in the cilantro. Serve immediately.

Makes 3 servings

Per serving: 191 calories, 28 g protein, 6 g carbohydrates, 5 g fat (less than 1 g saturated), 67 mg cholesterol, 1 g fiber, 308 mg sodium

NEW ORLEANS RUBBED CHICKEN WITH APRICOT-MUSTARD SAUCE

If you're a fan of spicy food, this one's for you. In fact, it's probably the spiciest dish in the book—and because it's coupled with the sweetness of apricot preserves, it's one of my favorites. If you're single like me, make only half or one-fourth of the sauce, then refrigerate the leftover chicken breasts. Serve them chopped over your favorite salad or slice them thinly and use in a wrap. The spicy kick will add punch and flavor and enliven subsequent meals.

---

1 tablespoon dried thyme

1½ teaspoons ground black pepper

1 teaspoon garlic powder

½ to 1 teaspoon cayenne, to taste

⅛ teaspoon salt

4 small (¼-pound) boneless, skinless chicken breasts, trimmed of visible fat

1 teaspoon extra-virgin olive oil

⅓ cup apricot 100% fruit preserves

2 tablespoons spicy brown mustard

Preheat the grill to high heat.

In a small bowl, combine the thyme, black pepper, garlic powder, cayenne, and salt. Mix to blend.

Place the chicken on a large plate or platter. Drizzle with the oil. Rub to coat both sides of the chicken evenly with the oil. Sprinkle the reserved seasoning mixture over both sides of the chicken. Rub to coat evenly. Cover with plastic wrap. Refrigerate for at least 10 minutes for the seasonings to flavor the chicken.

Meanwhile, spoon the preserves into a small microwaveable bowl. Cook on low power in 15-second intervals until melted. Stir in the mustard until well blended. Set aside.

Place the chicken on the grill and reduce the heat to medium. (If it is not possible to reduce the heat, cook the chicken away from direct heat.) Cook for 3 to 5 minutes per side, or until no longer pink and the juices run clear. Serve each breast with 2½ tablespoons of the reserved sauce spooned over the top.

Makes 4 servings

Per serving: 197 calories, 26 g protein, 15 g carbohydrates, 3 g fat (less than 1 g saturated), 66 mg cholesterol, 1 g fiber, 245 mg sodium

WINNING "FRIED" CHICKEN

I love this "fried" chicken because it's incredibly versatile. It's not only great as is, it's an awesome base for chicken Parmesan—simply add a bit of marinara sauce and some low-fat mozzarella cheese. I also love chopping it up to top a salad that is drizzled with a bit of wing sauce (just be careful of the sodium on that one). Oh, and in case you are wondering, panko is Japanese bread crumbs that are super crispy. They are ideal for faux fried foods because you don't need to add oil to achieve perfectly crisp breading. If you can't find panko, a second choice is crushed up Wasa crispbread, though I definitely prefer the panko.

3 tablespoons fat-free plain yogurt

4 large fresh basil leaves, chopped

1 teaspoon chopped fresh oregano leaves

1 teaspoon chopped fresh thyme leaves

¼ teaspoon garlic powder

Pinch of salt

Pinch of ground black pepper

4 tablespoons Ian's Whole Wheat Panko Breadcrumbs or finely crushed Wasa Light Rye Crispbread

2 small (¼-pound) boneless, skinless chicken breasts, trimmed of visible fat

Mustard or low-fat, low-sodium marinara sauce, to taste (optional)

Preheat the oven to 400°F. Lightly mist a small nonstick baking sheet with olive oil spray.

In a medium shallow bowl, combine the yogurt, basil, oregano, thyme, garlic powder, salt, and pepper. Stir to mix well.

Place 2 tablespoons of the bread crumbs or crushed crispbread in another medium shallow bowl. Set next to the yogurt mixture. Dip 1 chicken breast into the yogurt mixture to coat. Transfer to the crumbs to coat evenly. Place on the prepared baking sheet. Add the remaining 2 tablespoons crumbs to the bowl. Repeat the procedure with the second breast. Place on the baking sheet, not touching the other breast.

Bake for 10 minutes. Flip the chicken and bake for 8 to 10 minutes, or until no longer pink. Serve immediately with mustard or marinara sauce on the side, if desired.

Makes 2 servings

Per serving: 173 calories, 29 g protein, 9 g carbohydrates, 2 g fat (less than 1 g saturated), 66 mg cholesterol, 1 g fiber, 171 mg sodium

LORI'S LEAN LEMON CHICKEN

Lori Groat, member of the Biggest Loser Club (www.biggestloserclub. com), loves this chicken. "Put a garnish on your plate and serve the chicken with raw or cooked veggies," she says. The leftover chicken works well chopped up in salads or sliced very thinly for wraps or sandwiches. After it's cooked, simply remove it from the pan or dish, leaving the excess juices behind and chill.

2   teaspoons garlic powder

2   teaspoons lemon pepper seasoning blend, or to taste

½   teaspoon seasoned salt

4   small (¼-pound) boneless, skinless chicken breasts, trimmed of visible fat

    I Can't Believe It's Not Butter! spray

1   cup lemon juice, preferably fresh squeezed (4 or 5 lemons)

4   slices lemon

Preheat the oven to 400°F. Lightly mist an 8" x 8" glass or nonstick baking dish with olive oil spray.

In a small bowl, combine the garlic powder, lemon pepper, and seasoned salt. Mix to blend. Place the chicken on a large plate or platter. Rub the seasoning mixture evenly over the chicken. Cover with plastic wrap. Refrigerate for 15 minutes for the seasonings to flavor the chicken.

Place a large nonstick skillet over high heat until it is hot enough for a spritz of water to sizzle on it. With an oven mitt, briefly remove the pan from the heat to mist lightly with olive oil spray. Place the chicken in the pan. Cook for 2 to 3 minutes per side, or until browned. Place the chicken, smooth sides up and not overlapping, in the prepared baking dish. Spray each breast with 2 spritzes of I Can't Believe It's Not Butter! spray. Pour the lemon juice over the chicken. Top each breast with a lemon slice.

Bake for 21 to 24 minutes, or until no longer pink and the juices run clear. Remove from the oven. Baste with the pan juices. Let stand for 5 minutes before serving.

Makes 4 servings

Per serving: 147 calories, 27 g protein, 7 g carbohydrates, 1 g fat (trace saturated), 66 mg cholesterol, less than 1 g fiber, 353 mg sodium

Shown with Cajun "Squash Your Waistline" Fries, page 128

PECAN-CRUSTED CHICKEN

Though it is best not to overindulge in nuts because of their high fat content, they are great in small quantities as they've been found to lower cholesterol levels. I love this dish because it contains just enough pecans to really taste and enjoy them without adding an exorbitant amount of fat or calories. Store any remaining pecans in the freezer; they'll stay fresh there, and you won't be tempted to over-munch on them—even if you love them as much as I do.

1 large egg white

2 tablespoons minced toasted pecans

1 teaspoon chopped fresh parsley leaves

¼ teaspoon salt

2 small (¼-pound) boneless, skinless chicken breasts, trimmed of visible fat

Low-sugar, low-fat honey mustard salad dressing or Dijon mustard to taste (optional)

Preheat the oven to 350°F. Lightly mist a small nonstick baking sheet with olive oil spray.

In a small, shallow bowl, beat the egg white with a fork.

In a small bowl, combine the pecans, parsley, and salt. Spread half of the mixture on a sheet of waxed paper. Dip 1 chicken breast into the egg white to coat. Place the smooth side of the breast on the nut mixture. Press to adhere. Place the breast, nut side up, on the prepared baking sheet. Repeat with the second breast and place on the baking sheet, not touching the other breast.

Bake for 20 minutes or until no longer pink. Let stand 5 minutes. Serve with honey mustard dressing or Dijon mustard for dipping, if desired.

Makes 2 servings

Per serving: **183 calories, 28 g protein, 1 g carbohydrates, 7 g fat (less than 1 g saturated), 66 mg cholesterol, less than 1 fiber, 379 mg sodium**

To toast the pecans, spread them in a single layer on a small non-stick baking sheet. Place on the top rack in a preheated 350°F oven. Bake, watching closely, for 2 to 4 minutes, or until lightly browned. Remove and let stand to cool.

SOUTHWESTERN CHICKEN PILEUP

Sometimes, particularly when I'm trying to save calories, I really appreciate a meal that falls all over the place and definitely requires a napkin—unless I'm on a date! There's something about food being messy that makes it feel decadent. Here is a perfect example. With only 350 calories and 6 grams of fat, this pile of fresh ingredients atop a virtual pizza crust is definitely one to be savored.

1   teaspoon salt-free Mexican or Southwest seasoning

¼   teaspoon garlic powder

1   small (¼-pound) boneless, skinless chicken breast, trimmed of visible fat

1   whole-wheat pita (6½" diameter)

2   tablespoons hummus, preferably red-pepper flavor

2   tablespoons no-salt-added canned black beans, drained

Several red onion strips

Several red bell pepper strips

2   tablespoons chopped tomato

2   tablespoons chopped fresh cilantro leaves

2   tablespoons finely shredded Cabot 75% Light Cheddar Cheese

4   teaspoons guacamole or fat-free sour cream (optional)

Preheat the oven to 450°F. Preheat a grill to high heat.

Sprinkle the seasoning and garlic powder evenly over the chicken. Place the chicken on the grill rack. Reduce the heat to medium. (If it is not possible to reduce the heat, cook the chicken away from direct heat.) Grill for 3 to 5 minutes per side, or until no longer pink and the juices run clear. Transfer to a cutting board and let stand for 5 minutes. Chop the chicken into bite-sized pieces. Set aside.

Meanwhile, place the pita on the grill rack. Cook for 1 to 2 minutes per side, or until lightly toasted. Place the pita on a nonstick baking sheet. Spread evenly with the hummus. Top evenly in layers with the beans, the reserved chicken, onion, red pepper, tomato, cilantro, and cheese.

Bake for 6 to 8 minutes, or until the cheese is melted. Let stand for 5 minutes. Transfer to a serving plate. Slice into 4 wedges. Top each wedge with a teaspoon of guacamole or sour cream, if desired.

Makes 1 serving

Per serving: 356 calories, 38 g protein, 38 g carbohydrates, 6 g fat (1 g saturated), 68 mg cholesterol, 8 g fiber, 489 mg sodium

BIG ROOBY'S ALMOST-FAMOUS SKILLET FAJITAS

A staple in Ruben Hernandez's diet throughout his weight-loss journey, this is his healthy version of the Mexican specialty. Ruben uses two tortillas per serving, but with lots of sodium per tortilla, I recommend using just one. That way, you still get a big serving of the yummy veggies and leave room (nutritionally) for the optional toppings.

---

2 whole-wheat flour, low-carb, tortillas (7½" diameter)

½ medium onion, cut into strips

1 large red or yellow bell pepper, cut into strips

½ large jalapeño chile pepper, minced

½ medium zucchini, cut into strips

1½ teaspoons crushed garlic

½ pound boneless, skinless chicken breasts, trimmed of visible fat and cut into strips

½ cup salsa, drained if watery

Low-fat cheese, fat-free sour cream, and/or avocado, to taste (optional)

Preheat the oven to 400°F. Stack the tortillas on a large sheet of aluminum foil. Roll the foil into a tube enclosing the tortillas. Seal the ends. Set aside.

Lightly mist a large nonstick skillet with olive oil spray. Set over medium-high heat. Add the onion, bell pepper, chile pepper, zucchini, and garlic. Cook, stirring occasionally, for 6 to 8 minutes, or until the vegetables are tender and the onion is lightly browned. Transfer the vegetables to a plate. Cover to keep warm. Mist the pan again with olive oil spray and return to set over medium-high heat. Add the chicken. Cook, stirring occasionally, for 2 to 4 minutes, or until the chicken is browned on the outside and no longer pink on the inside. Add the salsa and the reserved vegetable mixture to the pan. Reduce the heat to low. Cook for 2 to 3 minutes, or until warm.

Meanwhile, heat the tortillas in the oven for about 5 minutes, or until warm.

Unroll the tortillas and place one on a serving plate. Fill it with one-fourth of the filling. Place another one-fourth of the filling on the side of the fajita. Repeat with the remaining tortilla and filling. Serve immediately with cheese, sour cream, and/or avocado, if desired.

Makes 2 servings

Per serving: **254 calories, 32 g protein, 20 g carbohydrates, 4 g fat (less than 1 g saturated), 66 mg cholesterol, 5 g fiber, 570 mg sodium**

DR. JEFF'S BREADED TILAPIA

Dr. Jeff Levine loves eating this tilapia recipe after it's been drizzled with lemon or dipped in salsa. I like to add 1 teaspoon of salt-free seasoning or fish rub to the egg substitute before breading it. This fish is really good with a bit of homemade tartar sauce, which I make by mixing 1½ tablespoons of low-fat or fat-free mayonnaise with 1½ tablespoons of dill relish (the tartar sauce adds 67 calories and 3 g fat)." Dr. Jeff adds, "serve it with a side of spaghetti squash or whole grain couscous" and you're sure to love it as much as we do.

3 **Wasa Crisp 'n' Light 7-Grain Crispbreads or 3 Wasa Light Rye Crispbreads, crushed into fine crumbs**

2 **tablespoons egg substitute**

3 **medium-size tilapia fillets (about ¼ pound)**

   Lemon wedges or salsa, to taste (optional)

Place the crumbs in a medium shallow bowl. Place the egg substitute in another medium shallow bowl.

Dip one tilapia fillet into the egg until it is coated. Then dip into the crumb mixture to coat (there will be some left over). Repeat with remaining fillets.

Lightly mist a small nonstick pan with olive oil spray. Place it over medium-high heat until it is hot enough for a spritz of water to sizzle on it. Place the fillets in the pan. Cook for 2 minutes per side then reduce the heat to medium. Cook for 3 to 4 minutes per side, or until the fillets flake easily with a fork. Serve immediately with lemon wedges or salsa, if desired.

Makes 1 serving

Per serving: 188 calories, 27 g protein, 14 g carbohydrates, 3 g fat (less than 1 g saturated), 57 mg cholesterol, 3 g fiber, 144 mg sodium

Shown with Dana's Spinach and Feta Brown Rice, page 125

BBQ TURKEY BREAST ROAST

I love making this roast and/or the Rosemary-Grilled London Broil (page 159) on Sunday afternoons, then later in the week slicing them to use in sandwiches and salads, or even to cube them for healthy munching. This turkey is not only flavorful, but with 248 milligrams of sodium per serving, it's a very low-sodium option.

¼ teaspoon garlic powder

¼ teaspoon salt

¼ teaspoon ground black pepper

1½ pounds Jennie-O Turkey Store Boneless, Skinless Turkey Breast Roast

1 teaspoon extra-virgin olive oil

2 tablespoons barbecue sauce (7 grams carbs or less per 2 tablespoons)

¼ cup water

Preheat the oven to 350°F. Lightly mist an 8" x 8" glass baking dish or nonstick baking pan with olive oil spray. In a small bowl, combine the garlic powder, salt, and pepper.

Place the turkey on a cutting board. With a fork, pierce each side deeply about 25 times. Drizzle on the oil and rub to coat evenly on both sides. Sprinkle on the reserved seasoning mixture. Rub to coat evenly on both sides. With the smooth side of the breast down, drizzle on half of the barbecue sauce, rubbing to coat. Place the turkey, smooth side up, in the prepared pan. Rub the remaining barbecue sauce over the smooth side of the breast. Pour the water into the pan, taking care not to pour it over the turkey.

Bake for 35 to 40 minutes, or until a thermometer inserted in the thickest portion registers 160°F and the juices run clear.

Remove from the oven. Let stand for 10 minutes. Place the turkey on a clean cutting board. Carve, against the grain, into thin slices. Serve immediately.

Make 5 (4-ounce) servings

Per serving: 160 calories, 34 g protein, 2 g carbohydrates, 3 g fat (trace saturated), 54 mg cholesterol, trace fiber, 248 mg sodium

Slice only the portion you are eating for one meal and refrigerate the remainder. Just before using, slice the turkey as thinly as possible for sandwiches or cube it for munching or to use in salads.

HEATHER'S MEXICAN ROLLUP

Heather Hansen relies on this easy rollup to help toward her weight-loss goal. To keep from getting bored with it, she alternates between making it with Jennie-O Turkey Store Extra Lean Ground Turkey and extra-lean beef. Though she generally eats the turkey naked, I prefer to spike it with 1½ teaspoons of Mrs. Dash Southwest Chipotle Seasoning or other salt-free Mexican seasoning, which I mix into the meat before cooking. Either way, it's a great option for a quick dinner.

¼ pound Jennie-O Turkey Store Extra Lean Ground Turkey or extra-lean ground beef

1 whole-wheat flour, low-carb tortilla (7½" diameter)

1 tablespoon fat-free sour cream

⅓ cup shredded romaine lettuce leaves

⅓ cup seeded, chopped tomato

2 tablespoons thick-and-chunky mild, medium, or hot salsa

Place a small nonstick skillet on medium-high heat until it is hot enough for a spritz of water to sizzle on it. With an oven mitt, briefly remove the pan from the heat to mist lightly with oil spray. Add the turkey or beef to the pan. Cook, breaking into chunks with a wooden spoon for 3 to 4 minutes, or until lightly browned and no longer pink. Transfer the turkey or beef to a plate. Cover to keep warm.

Return the pan to medium heat. Place the tortilla in the pan. Cook for about 30 seconds per side, or until just warmed. Transfer to a serving plate.

Starting at one side, spread the sour cream evenly over two-thirds of the tortilla. Scatter the reserved turkey or beef over the sour cream. Top with the lettuce, tomato, and salsa. Starting at the filled end, roll the tortilla tightly into a tube, being careful not to tear it.

Serve immediately.

Makes 1 serving

Per serving: 234 calories, 34 g protein, 14 g carbohydrates, 4 g fat (less than 1 g saturated), 46 mg cholesterol, 5 g fat, 582 mg sodium

Shown with Hazelnut and Lemon Green Beans, page 136

PAN-"FRIED" CATFISH WITH SOUTHWEST TARTAR SAUCE

I love tartar sauce. In fact, if it weren't for tartar sauce, I'd enjoy most fish a lot less. Here I've created a twist on the standard by coupling mayo with Mexican seasonings. The richness of the seasonings eliminates the presence of any potential aftertaste from the mayonnaise, while the mayonnaise serves to delight the palate with contrasting texture and temperature. Yum.

1 tablespoon low-fat mayonnaise

1½ teaspoons chopped fresh cilantro leaves, plus additional leaves for garnish (optional)

1 teaspoon lime juice, preferably fresh squeezed

⅛ teaspoon ground chipotle chile pepper

1 small (¼-pound) catfish fillet

Pinch of paprika, or to taste

Pinch of garlic powder, or to taste

To prepare the tartar sauce: In a small bowl, combine the mayonnaise, cilantro, lime juice, and chipotle pepper. Mix well. Set aside.

Season both sides of the catfish evenly with the paprika and garlic powder. Set a small nonstick skillet over medium-high heat until it is hot enough for a spritz of water to sizzle on it. With an oven mitt, briefly remove the pan from the heat to lightly mist with olive oil spray. Place the catfish in the pan. Cook for 1 minute per side, or until seared. Reduce the heat to medium. Cook for 2 to 3 minutes per side, or until the catfish flakes easily. Transfer to a serving plate. Spoon the reserved tartar sauce over the top. Garnish with cilantro leaves, if desired. Serve immediately.

Makes 1 serving

Per serving: 136 calories, 19 g protein, 3 g carbohydrates, 5 g fat (1 g saturated), 66 mg cholesterol, trace fiber, 179 mg sodium

Catfish nuggets can also be used for this recipe but note that they will take only about 1 minute per side to cook.

BLACKENED CATFISH

If you're looking for a fresh dinner in a flash, you can't possibly go wrong with this dish. It takes only about 15 minutes to make, but you'd never guess from the taste. I buy catfish that has been flash frozen and keep it in my freezer. The night before or the morning of the day I plan to serve it, I move it to the fridge. By the time dinner hits, it's defrosted and ready to go. But if I forget to defrost it, it doesn't stress me out. I just run it under cold (not hot) water for about 10 minutes, and then lightly squeeze the moisture from it—it's ready to roll.

1 **small (¼-pound) catfish fillet**

¼ **teaspoon blackened seasoning, or more to taste**

½ **teaspoon grated reduced-fat Parmesan cheese**

Preheat the oven to 450°F. Lightly mist a small nonstick baking sheet with olive oil spray. Place the catfish, smooth-side down, on the sheet. Sprinkle on the blackened seasoning and cheese.

Bake for 10 to 12 minutes, or until the catfish flakes easily with a fork. Serve immediately.

Makes 1 serving

Per serving: **110 calories, 19 g protein, 0 g carbohydrates, 3 g fat (less than 1 g saturated), 66 mg cholesterol, 0 g fiber, 165 mg sodium**

MATT HOOVER

Remember, if you like to eat a lot of food, you can eat more healthy food than junk food for the same number of calories.

PAN-"FRIED" JERK SALMON WITH TANGY APRICOT SAUCE

This is another dish that's great if you don't have a lot of time. If you're intimidated by the notion of purchasing fresh fish, don't be. Just remember that fish should never smell "fishy" or feel slimy. Sure, it will have a mild fish-like odor, but it shouldn't actually be fishy. Also, look carefully at fillets before you purchase them. They should have a bright color throughout. If the edges are looking pale or dull in color, you may want to head to the frozen fish aisle to make your purchase.

1½ tablespoons 100% apricot fruit preserves

1 teaspoon prepared horseradish

1 teaspoon jerk seasoning or rub

1 small (¼-pound) boneless, skinless salmon fillet

Spoon the preserves into a small microwaveable bowl. Microwave on low power in 15 second intervals until hot. Stir in the horseradish. Set aside.

Rub the seasoning into the salmon to coat all sides.

Place a small nonstick skillet over medium-high heat until it is hot enough for a spritz of water to sizzle on it. With an oven mitt, briefly remove the pan from the heat to lightly mist with olive oil spray.

Place the salmon in the pan, smooth side down. Cook for 2 minutes per side. Reduce the heat to medium. Cook for 2 to 3 minutes per side, or until the salmon is opaque. Transfer to a serving plate. Spoon the reserved sauce over the salmon. Serve immediately.

Makes 1 serving

Per serving: 270 calories, 23 g protein, 16 g carbohydrates, 12 g fat (2 g saturated), 67 mg cholesterol, trace g fiber, 363 mg sodium

MUSTARD AND HERB–BAKED SALMON

This is one of my all-time favorite salmon dishes to chill and serve over a salad. That said, however, it's also excellent hot. If you are generally too tired after a long day of work to chop herbs, prep this dish in the morning before work, and then store the fillets in an airtight plastic container in the refrigerator. When you get home, you'll just have to pop it in the oven and voila, *dinner without any fuss. To save some money, you might consider visiting a local farmers' market to buy your herbs.*

10   fresh tarragon leaves

3   fresh chives

3   large fresh basil leaves

1   tablespoon fresh flat-leaf parsley leaves

1   small (¼-pound) boneless, skinless salmon fillet

2   teaspoons spicy brown or Dijon mustard

Preheat the oven to 400°F. Lightly mist a small nonstick baking sheet with olive oil spray.

In a food processor fitted with a chopping blade, combine the tarragon, chives, basil, and parsley. Process until finely chopped (or chop by hand). Place the salmon in the prepared pan. Brush or rub the mustard over the salmon. Sprinkle evenly with the herb mixture, then press it into the mustard. Lightly mist with olive oil spray.

Bake for 11 to 13 minutes, or until the salmon is opaque. Serve hot or chilled.

Makes 1 serving

> **Per serving:** 215 calories, 23 g protein, less than 1 g carbohydrates, 13 g fat (2 g saturated), 67 mg cholesterol, trace g fiber, 200 mg sodium

TRAINER TIP: **BOB HARPER**

Find things that you like to eat in restaurants. Chinese food isn't all stir-fried and fat. You can get anything you want steamed with that sauce on the side, and then you are able to manage how many calories you put on it.

DEE'S SPICY ORANGE ROUGHY

Dee Dennis, member of the Biggest Loser Club (www.biggestloserclub. com), sent us this quick and easy recipe. If you want to change it up, you can use tilapia instead of orange roughy. Both types of fish are widely available frozen, making this recipe a cinch to prepare any time.

1 small (¼-pound) orange roughy fillet

1 teaspoon jerk seasoning, or more to taste

⅛ teaspoon cayenne, or more to taste

1 teaspoon extra-virgin olive oil

Place the orange roughy on a sheet of waxed paper. Sprinkle one side evenly with half of the jerk seasoning followed by half of the cayenne.

Place a medium nonstick skillet over medium heat. Add the oil. Heat for about 30 seconds, or until hot. Place the orange roughy, seasoned side down, in the pan. Sprinkle the remaining seasonings over the top. Cook for 3 to 4 minutes per side, or until the orange roughy flakes easily. Serve immediately.

Makes 1 serving

Per serving: 129 calories, 19 g protein, trace carbohydrates, 6 g fat (less than 1 g saturated), 68 mg cholesterol, trace fiber, 362 mg sodium

ANGEL HAIR WITH ROCKIN' RED CLAM SAUCE

Though I'm Italian, I'd stopped eating pasta for years. But a few years back, I discovered Nutrition Kitchen's soy pasta, which is like no other I've found. It's made from 100 percent organic soybeans, has 11 grams of fiber and 23 grams of protein per serving . . . for pasta! Though I don't even like soybeans, once I add a sauce, I find the pasta to be so satisfying; it's a must-have staple in my home. I like this pasta al dente—so I only cook it for 3 minutes. Oh, and one other note: Traditional red clam sauce tends to have a stronger garlic flavor than this one does. If you want that strong garlic taste, definitely add more, but we enjoy it just like this.

Salt

1½ tablespoons finely chopped yellow or white onion

2 small cloves garlic, minced

1 pouch (3½ ounces) baby clams, drained

½ cup canned crushed tomatoes

½ teaspoon dried oregano leaves

½ teaspoon extra-virgin olive oil

Pinch of red-pepper flakes, or more to taste

2 ounces (one-fourth of an 8-ounce box) Nutrition Kitchen Angel Hair Style Golden Whole Soybean Pasta

1 to 2 teaspoons grated reduced-fat Parmesan cheese

Bring a large pot of lightly salted water to a boil.

Meanwhile, lightly mist a small nonstick skillet with olive oil spray. Set over medium heat. Add the onion and garlic. Cook, stirring occasionally, for about 4 minutes, or until almost tender. (Do not brown.) Add the clams. Increase the heat to medium high. Cook for 2 to 3 minutes, or until the excess liquid is completely evaporated. Reduce the heat to low. Add the tomatoes, oregano, and oil. Season with red-pepper flakes.

Meanwhile, when the water boils, add the pasta to the pot. Stir. Cook, stirring occasionally, for 3 minutes, or until al dente. Drain and add to the skillet mixture. Toss to combine. Transfer to a serving bowl. Sprinkle with the cheese. Serve immediately.

Makes 1 serving

Per serving: **392 calories, 42 g protein, 40 g carbohydrates, 9 g fat (2 g saturated), 82 mg cholesterol, 14 g fiber, 726 mg sodium**

INDIVIDUAL SAUSAGE-RIGATONI BAKE

I grew up eating sausage and peppers and tons of other sausage-infused Italian favorites. When I started dieting, I thought I had to say good-bye to sausage forever. But later I figured out that I could season the leanest cut of pork just like sweet Italian sausage. Now I eat it all of the time as long as I make it myself . . . and you can, too!

SAUSAGE

- 3 ounces extra-lean ground pork
- ½ teaspoon fennel seeds
- ½ teaspoon dried parsley
- ¼ teaspoon red-pepper flakes
- ¼ teaspoon Italian seasoning
- ⅛ teaspoon garlic powder
  Pinch of salt

RIGATONI AND SAUCE

- ¾ cup whole-wheat rigatoni
- ⅔ cup thin, 1"-long red or yellow bell pepper strips
- 1 cup canned crushed tomatoes
- 1 tablespoon no-salt-added tomato paste
- 1 tablespoon water
- 1½ teaspoons dried oregano
- ½ teaspoon honey
- ¼ teaspoon garlic powder
- 2 teaspoons grated reduced-fat Parmesan cheese

Preheat the oven to 400°F.

To prepare the sausage: Combine the pork, fennel seeds, parsley, pepper flakes, Italian seasoning, garlic powder, and salt. With clean hands or a fork, mix well.

Place a medium nonstick skillet over medium-high heat until it is hot enough for a spritz of water to sizzle on it. With an oven mitt, briefly remove the pan from the heat to lightly mist with olive oil spray.

Add the sausage to the pan. Cook, breaking it into large chunks with a wooden spoon, for 3 to 5 minutes, or until no longer pink. Remove from the pan and cover to keep warm.

To prepare the rigatoni and sauce: Lightly mist a 2- to 3-cup baking dish with olive oil spray. Set aside.

Cook the pasta according to package directions. Drain and set aside.

Meanwhile, return the skillet to the heat, add the pepper strips, and cook 3 to 5 minutes until tender. Add the reserved sausage. Add tomatoes, tomato paste, water, oregano, honey, and garlic powder. Stir to mix well. Add the reserved pasta. Transfer to the prepared baking dish. Sprinkle evenly with the cheese. Cover with aluminum foil.

Bake for 10 minutes. Remove the aluminum foil. Bake for 5 minutes, or until heated through and the top is starting to brown. Let stand for 5 minutes before serving.

Makes 1 serving

Per serving: 427 calories, 30 g protein, 66 g carbohydrates, 7 g fat (1 g saturated), 60 mg cholesterol, 12 g fiber, 629 mg sodium

MUSCLING-UP MEATBALLS

People are often surprised to learn that store-bought sausage and meatballs made from chicken or turkey usually get 50 percent or more of their calories from fat. That's why I always make my own. This recipe is one of my favorites. I'm pretty sure you'll find these meatballs worthy of adding to your favorite Italian dishes . . . and your guests (and kids!) will never suspect that they're low-anything. Also try them in Superior Spaghetti and Meatballs (page 190), Ryan's Open-Faced Meatball Sandwich (page 108), or on your favorite pizza. If you can't find extra-lean ground chicken, ask your butcher to grind chicken breasts for you. They'll do it free of charge at most major grocery stores . . . if you ask nicely, that is.

¾ **cup Ian's Whole Wheat Panko Breadcrumbs or lightly crushed Wasa Light Rye Crispbread**

⅓ **cup fat-free milk**

1 **pound extra-lean ground chicken**

3 **large egg whites**

¼ **cup chopped fresh parsley leaves**

1 **tablespoon plus 1 teaspoon grated reduced-fat Parmesan cheese**

2 **teaspoons garlic powder**

2 **teaspoons onion powder**

½ **teaspoon salt**

Preheat the oven to 400°F. Lightly mist a medium baking sheet with olive oil spray. Set aside.

In a mixing bowl, combine the bread crumbs or crushed crispbread and the milk. Let stand for 2 to 3 minutes, or until the milk softens the crumbs. Add the chicken, egg whites, parsley, cheese, garlic powder, onion powder, and salt. With clean hands or a fork, mix well. Divide the mixture into 16 equal pieces. Roll each piece between your palms to shape into a ball. Place the meatballs, not touching, on the prepared baking sheet.

Bake for 12 to 15 minutes, or until no longer pink inside.

Makes 16 meatballs

Per meatball: 55 calories, 8 g protein, 4 g carbohydrates, less than 1 g fat (trace saturated), 17 mg cholesterol, trace fiber, 119 mg sodium

If you're using the meatballs in a soup or in a dish where smaller meatballs would work better, use a 1¼" cookie scoop or 2 tablespoons to form 1¼" meatballs. Reduce the baking time to 8 to 10 minutes. Makes about 24 meatballs.

AMANDA'S CHEESY EGGPLANT LASAGNA

Though Amanda Carlson confessed to me that it's actually her husband who makes this recipe, it's one of her all-time favorites. She swears that "it tastes sinful even though it's low in calories." Amanda's husband also sometimes adds cooked Jennie-O Turkey Store Extra Lean Ground Turkey and Italian seasonings, which he layers in after the mushrooms.

2 medium eggplants, peeled and cut into ¼"-thick lengthwise slices

2 pinches of garlic salt, or to taste

1 package (8 ounces or more, to taste) sliced fresh mushrooms

1 clove garlic, minced

2 cups low-fat marinara sauce

1¾ cups (6 ounces) finely shredded low-fat or fat-free mozzarella cheese

Preheat the broiler. Mist a 13" x 9" glass baking dish with olive oil spray. Set aside.

Lightly mist the eggplant with olive oil spray. Place on a medium nonstick baking sheet. Sprinkle both sides with garlic salt. Broil 6" from the heat source for 3 to 5 minutes per side, or until tender.

Meanwhile, lightly mist a medium nonstick skillet with olive oil spray. Set over medium heat. Add the mushrooms and garlic. Cook, stirring occasionally, for 8 to 10 minutes, or until there is no liquid remaining in the pan and the mushrooms are starting to brown.

Preheat the oven to 350°F. Place half of the eggplant in a single layer in the bottom of the prepared baking dish. Top with half of the mushroom mixture, half of the marinara sauce, and half of the cheese. Repeat with the remaining eggplant, mushrooms, sauce, and cheese. Cover with aluminum foil.

Bake for 20 minutes. Remove the aluminum foil. Bake for 10 to 15 minutes, or until hot and the cheese is bubbly. Remove and let stand for 10 minutes. Cut into 6 equal portions. Serve immediately.

Makes 6 servings

Per serving: **196 calories, 16 g protein, 25 g carbohydrates, 5 g fat (2 g saturated), 15 mg cholesterol, 11 g fiber, 800 mg sodium**

SUPERIOR SPAGHETTI AND MEATBALLS

When I was a kid, I had a "spaghetti shirt"—a red shirt dedicated solely to eating spaghetti (and other Italian dishes) so I didn't ruin my other clothes. The days I'd arrive home from school to hear my mom say, "Go put on your spaghetti shirt," I always knew we were in for a treat. Though my updated version of my childhood favorite doesn't have as much fat or as many calories, I look forward to it just as much. And, of course, it's just as sloppy, so that I never indulge in it while wearing clothes that require dry-cleaning. You might not want to, either.

Salt

2 ounces (one-fourth of an 8-ounce box) Nutrition Kitchen Angel Hair Style Golden Soybean Pasta

¾ cup Superior Spaghetti Sauce (opposite page), heated

2 Muscling-Up Meatballs (page 188), heated

2 teaspoons grated reduced-fat Parmesan cheese (optional)

Bring a large pot of lightly salted water to a boil. Add the pasta to the pot. Stir. Cook, stirring occasionally, for 3 minutes, or until al dente. Drain. Transfer to a pasta bowl or serving plate. Top with the sauce and meatballs. Sprinkle with the cheese, if desired.

Makes 1 serving

Per serving: **446 calories, 44 g protein, 52 g carbohydrates, 8 g fat (2 g saturated), 39 mg cholesterol, 16 g fiber, 578 mg sodium**

SUPERIOR SPAGHETTI SAUCE

This spaghetti sauce is a great replacement for store-bought sauce, which can have more than 600 milligrams of sodium per serving. It also freezes well, so you can keep some on hand for a fast weeknight dinner.

⅓ cup finely chopped yellow or white onion

2 teaspoons minced garlic

1⅓ cups canned crushed tomatoes

1 tablespoon no-salt-added tomato paste

1 tablespoon water

1 teaspoon honey

1 teaspoon dried oregano leaves

1 teaspoon Italian seasoning

1 teaspoon extra-virgin olive oil

½ teaspoon dried basil leaves

Lightly mist a medium nonstick saucepan with olive oil spray. Set over medium heat. Add the onion and garlic. Cook, stirring occasionally, for 3 to 5 minutes, or until almost tender (do not brown). Reduce the heat to low. Add the tomatoes, tomato paste, water, honey, oregano, Italian seasoning, olive oil, and basil. Stir with a wooden spoon to mix. Simmer for 5 minutes for the flavors to blend.

Makes 3 (½-cup) servings

Per serving: 76 calories, 2 g protein, 14 g carbohydrates, 2 g fat (trace saturated), 0 mg cholesterol, 3 g fiber, 170 mg sodium

JEFF LEVINE

Before you put something in your mouth, ask yourself "Am I hungry?" Recognize your specific food and eating triggers and develop strategies to modify, limit, or avoid them.

DAVE'S TERIYAKI TOFU

One of Dave Fioravanti's favorite things is cooking. He rarely follows recipes. Instead, "I just throw things together," he says. "If people knew how great healthy food could taste, that's all they'd eat." Because Dave is usually in a hurry, he makes this dish using only tofu, teriyaki sauce, garlic, olive oil, and red pepper flakes. I like grabbing a few extra ingredients to make it even more special, as I do below!

1 package (12 ounces) light firm tofu, drained and cut into 1" cubes

3 whole green onions, finely chopped

1 teaspoon minced fresh garlic

1 teaspoon minced fresh ginger

½ teaspoon extra-virgin olive oil

¼ teaspoon hot sesame oil

1 cup chopped fresh broccoli

2 tablespoons light teriyaki sauce

⅛ teaspoon red-pepper flakes, or more to taste

Place a nonstick wok or skillet over high heat until it is hot enough for a spritz of water to sizzle on it. With an oven mitt, briefly remove the pan from the heat to lightly mist with olive oil spray. Heat for 3 seconds. Add the tofu, green onions, garlic, ginger, olive oil, and sesame oil. Cook, stirring often, for 3 minutes. Add the broccoli. Cook, stirring frequently, for about 12 minutes, or until the tofu is browned on all sides. Stir in the teriyaki sauce. Season with pepper flakes. Cook for 30 to 60 seconds, or until the sauce thickens slightly. Spoon onto 2 serving plates. Serve immediately.

Makes 2 servings

Per serving: **118 calories, 13 g protein, 10 g carbohydrates, 3 g fat (less than 1 g saturated), 0 mg cholesterol, 2 g fiber, 597 mg sodium**

9

Sweet Snacks

There's no denying that most of us have a fearsome sweet tooth. It's one of the hardest things to reckon with when trying to lose weight. But we've got some good news for you: The recipes in this chapter will satisfy your sweet tooth, whether you're enjoying the treats as midday snacks or as after-dinner desserts.

We all know that traditional desserts and sweet snacks are fattening—but it's not just the calorie count in a chocolate doughnut that makes it hard to reach your weight-loss goals. Most sweets are filled with white sugar and white flour, which are appetite stimulators. These ingredients have been stripped of their fiber and, when digested, the sugar and refined starch cause your blood sugar to skyrocket. In response, your body overreacts, pumping out so much insulin that your blood sugar plummets. When your blood sugar is low, you feel tired, cranky, hungry, and in need of a quick food fix, often in the form of something sweet. And *voila*—there's the vicious circle that wreaks havoc on your diet.

The key, of course, is to avoid appetite-stimulating foods and reach for natural, wholesome items instead. But that doesn't mean that the sweet snacks in this chapter will taste like "health food." What's not to love about Peanut Butter–Oatmeal Cookies, Chocolate-Kahlúa Mousse Parfaits, and Lisa's Frozen Gramwiches?

Fruits are naturally sweet and they can be made into fabulous sweet snacks. You'll learn to wrap your taste buds around some new sensations, like Blackberry Sorbet–Filled Lemon Cups and Pumpkin-Walnut Snack Muffins. Bottom line: The snacks in this chapter won't let your sweet tooth down.

PEANUT BUTTER–OATMEAL COOKIES

Peanut butter cookies in a healthy cookbook? Yep! I love these no-bake cookies made with dates—and the cool part is that the sugars found in dates are natural sugars that your body can easily process. Though you still don't want to eat a whole container of the cookies, when enjoyed in moderation they definitely curb a sweet tooth and a peanut butter craving all at once.

12 pitted dates

⅓ cup old fashioned oats

1 tablespoon reduced-fat peanut butter

Place the dates in the bowl of a mini-food processor fitted with the chopping blade. Process until the dates are very finely chopped and stick together. With a spatula, transfer to a small mixing bowl. Add the oats and peanut butter. Using an electric mixer fitted with beaters or your hands, mix well.

Divide the mixture into 4 equal amounts. Shape each into a ball. Place one ball between two sheets of waxed paper. Flatten the ball to a 3" diameter cookie. Repeat with each ball. Serve immediately or stack between sheets of waxed paper in an airtight plastic container. Refrigerate for up to 5 days.

Makes 2 (2-cookie) servings

Per serving: 221 calories, 5 g protein, 45 g carbohydrates, 4 g fat (less than 1 g saturated), 0 mg cholesterol, 5 g fiber, 63 mg sodium

TRAINER TIP: **KIM LYONS**

Moderate your alcohol use, since alcoholic beverages are loaded with sugary calories which are easily converted to fat.

ONE-SERVING CHOCOLATE CHEESECAKES

I prefer to make desserts in single-serving sizes. It helps me with portion control (and hopefully it will help you, too). When I'm faced with an entire cheesecake, I tend to feel justified in having "just another sliver," but I'd never dream of breaking into a second dessert—well, almost never . . . But nobody's perfect, right?

I Can't Believe It's Not Butter! spray

¼ cup crunchy high-fiber, low-sugar cereal (such as Grape-Nuts), finely crushed into crumbs

½ cup fat-free cream cheese, at room temperature

2 tablespoons honey

1 large egg white

¼ cup fat-free, artificially sweetened vanilla yogurt

¼ teaspoon vanilla extract

¼ cup cocoa powder, plus more for garnish

4 tablespoons aerosol fat-free whipped topping

Preheat the oven to 350°F.

Lightly mist four 3"-wide ovenproof bowls or ramekins with I Can't Believe It's Not Butter! spray. Divide the crumbs among them, spreading in an even layer on the bottoms. Set aside.

In a small mixing bowl, with an electric mixer fitted with beaters, beat the cream cheese and honey on medium speed until smooth. Add the egg white, yogurt, and vanilla. Beat on medium speed just until smooth. On the lowest speed possible, mix in the cocoa. Spoon the mixture into the prepared bowls or ramekins.

Bake for 12 to 15 minutes, or until the centers are set. Let stand for 15 minutes to cool. Refrigerate for at least 2 hours. Just before serving, top each serving with a tablespoon of whipped topping. Dust with cocoa.

Makes 4 servings

Per serving: **107 calories, 5 g protein, 21 g carbohydrates, 1 g fat (less than 1 g saturated), 1 mg cholesterol, 2 g fiber, 149 mg sodium**

Try not to "whip" the cheesecake mixture on too high of a speed, or the finished cakes will get cracks in the top. Be sure to beat it on medium speed until just combined.

TROPICAL ESCAPE SMOOTHIE

This is another recipe that I love to serve in a fancy glass, like a jumbo martini or wine glass. Whether I'm in my kitchen or off sunbathing on a tropical island, food always seems more decadent and tasty when it looks pretty. If possible, buy a whole pineapple every once in awhile, then chop it up and freeze it. It will always be ready to go and tastes much better than canned pineapple.

1   cup pineapple chunks, frozen

½   medium ripe banana

½   cup fat-free vanilla soy milk

In the jar of a blender, combine the pineapple, banana, and milk. Blend on high speed or ice-crush setting for 30 to 60 seconds, or until smooth. Pour into a glass. Serve immediately.

Makes 1 serving

Per serving: 162 calories, 5 g protein, 38 g carbohydrates, less than 1 g fat (trace saturated), 0 mg cholesterol, 2 g fiber, 55 mg sodium

MARTY'S CREAMY PINEAPPLE SORBET

Marty Wolff was big on going to the local hangouts to order his favorite grub: "Hot fudge shakes, baby back ribs, barbecue, and twice-baked potatoes . . . and all extra-large portions." Now that he's on the ranch, he's trying to ease himself into eating a lot more fruits and veggies. And he found this sorbet to be a great substitute for his ice cream treats. "I can eat a good-sized portion because it's really light and isn't packed with sugar."

1½ cups pineapple chunks, frozen

⅓ cup fat-free, artificially sweetened piña colada, coconut, or vanilla yogurt

1 teaspoon lemon juice, preferably fresh-squeezed

1 to 2 packets (0.35 ounces each) sugar substitute (such as Splenda), to taste (optional)

Place the pineapple in the bowl of a food processor fitted with a chopping blade. Pulse, scraping down the sides of the bowl as needed, until finely chopped. Add the yogurt and lemon juice. Process, scraping down the sides of the bowl again, until very smooth. Stir in the sugar substitute, if desired. Spoon into 2 martini glasses or dessert bowls. Serve immediately.

Makes 2 (⅔-cup) servings

Per serving: 78 calories, 2 g protein, 19 g carbohydrates, trace fat (trace saturated), less than 1 mg cholesterol, 2 g fiber, 23 mg sodium

BLACKBERRY SORBET–FILLED LEMON CUPS

Though extremely light, this dessert is definitely impressive enough to serve to guests. If you're pressed for time, skip the lemon cups and serve the sorbet in martini glasses.

6 lemons

2 cups frozen unsweetened blackberries (not thawed), plus 6 blackberries for garnish (optional)

½ cup fat-free, artificially sweetened vanilla or berry yogurt

1½ teaspoons lemon juice, preferably fresh-squeezed

1 packet (0.35 ounce) sugar substitute (such as Splenda), or to taste (optional)

From a lemon, cut a slice from the stem end that is about one-fifth of the size of the fruit. Cut a sliver of peel from the opposite end so the lemon will sit upright. Repeat with the remaining lemons. With a serrated knife, kitchen scissors, and citrus spoon, carefully scoop out all the flesh from the lemons, keeping the peel intact. (Reserve the juice and pulp for another recipe.) Place the shells in a plastic storage container or resealable plastic freezer bag. Freeze for at least 3 hours or as long as overnight.

Just before serving, place the berries in the bowl of a food processor fitted with a chopping blade. Pulse, scraping down the sides of the bowl as needed, until finely chopped. Add the yogurt and lemon juice; process, again scraping down the sides of the bowl as needed, until very smooth. Sweeten with sugar substitute, if desired. Spoon the sorbet into the reserved lemon shells. Garnish each with a berry, if desired. Serve immediately.

Makes 6 (¼-cup) servings

Per serving: **43 calories, 1 g protein, 10 g carbohydrates, trace fat (trace saturated), less than 1 mg cholesterol, 3 g fiber, 11 mg sodium**

ICED BUFFED MOCHA

If you're guilty of hitting the nearest coffee empire for a chocolaty frozen coffee jolt, you're not alone. Not only will this recipe satisfy your craving in the privacy of your own home, it is likely to save you a significant amount of cash over time . . . oh, and fat and calories, too!

1 tablespoon water

¾ teaspoon instant coffee powder

1 cup light chocolate soy milk

2 tablespoons fat-free, artificially sweetened vanilla yogurt

1 packet (0.35 ounce) sugar substitute (such as Splenda)

8 ice cubes

2 tablespoons aerosol fat-free whipped topping (optional)

Cocoa powder (optional)

In a small microwaveable cup, combine the water and coffee powder. Microwave on high power for about 20 seconds, or until hot. Stir to dissolve the powder.

In the jar of a blender, combine the milk, yogurt, sugar substitute, reserved coffee mixture, and ice. Blend on high speed or ice-crush setting for 30 to 60 seconds, or until smooth. Pour into a large glass. Garnish with whipped topping and dust with cocoa, if desired. Serve immediately with a straw.

Makes 1 serving

Per serving: 127 calories, 9 g protein, 18 g carbohydrates, 2 g fat (less than 1 g saturated), 1 mg cholesterol, 1 g fiber, 223 mg sodium

TRAINER TIP: **BOB HARPER**

Sometimes working out means not even going to the gym. I find that if I have a couple of 10-pound weights, for instance, or even 5-pound weights in my house, I can do a workout.

FROZEN HOT CHOCOLATE

When I was 19, I dated a guy who took me to a restaurant in New York City where they served frozen hot chocolate. I don't remember the name of the restaurant. I really don't remember the guy. But I do remember the treat! My version, made with fat-free, sugar-free hot chocolate, is a great snack for those nights when you know you've eaten enough, but you just can't get chocolate off your mind. It's only 25 calories, yet it's satisfying and takes awhile to eat. Just be sure to make a few at a time so they're waiting in the freezer when the craving hits.

⅔ cup hot water

1 packet (.29 ounce) sugar-free, fat-free hot chocolate mix

2 tablespoons aerosol fat-free whipped topping (optional)

In a small freezer-safe plastic container with a lid, combine the water and chocolate mix. Stir or whisk to dissolve the powder completely. Let stand to cool. Cover the container and place in the freezer for 4 to 5 hours, or until solid.

To serve, let the container stand at room temperature for 10 to 15 minutes, or until the hot chocolate is just starting to melt slightly around the edges. Or, place the container in the microwave and cook on high power for about 30 seconds. (It should still be somewhat hard and need to be scraped with a spoon.) Dollop with whipped topping, if desired. Serve immediately.

Makes 1 serving

Per serving: 25 calories, 2 g protein, 4 g carbohydrates, 0 g fat, 0 mg cholesterol, 1 g fiber, 150 mg sodium

KAI'S SWEET STRAWBERRY BOWL

Kai Hibbard deemed this treat her "favorite low-cal dessert." It's a twist on plain strawberries that reminds her of breakfast cereal, which happens to be her favorite evening snack. This recipe is particularly good in the summer months when strawberries are at their peak in sweetness—and when they tend to be less expensive.

1 cup sliced strawberries

¼ cup fat-free vanilla soy milk

1 packet (.035 ounce) sugar substitute (such as Splenda)

In a serving bowl, combine the strawberries, soy milk, and sugar substitute. Stir gently. Serve immediately.

Makes 1 serving

Per serving: 77 calories, 3 g protein, 17 g carbohydrates, less than 1 g fat (trace saturated), 0 mg cholesterol, 4 g fiber, 28 mg sodium

ERIK CHOPIN

A sugar-free Fudgsicle makes a great snack and can satisfy any chocolate urge.

WHITE CHOCOLATE–STRAWBERRY PIE-LETS

Most store-bought pie crusts are full of butter and refined sugars. Instead of indulging in those, I've found that adding 100% fruit preserves to finely crushed cereal crumbs creates a perfect alternative that adds plenty of flavor. Feel free to use raspberry preserves or another flavor of choice instead of the strawberry I suggest here.

½ cup crunchy high-fiber, low-sugar cereal (such as Grape-Nuts), finely crushed into crumbs

2 tablespoons plus 2 teaspoons strawberry 100% fruit preserves

1¾ cups fat-free milk

1 package (1 ounce) sugar-free, fat-free white chocolate pudding mix

In a small mixing bowl, combine the crumbs and 2 tablespoons of the preserves. With a large spoon, stir to mix well. Divide the mixture into 4 ramekins or small dessert bowls. Press the mixture into the bottom of the dishes. Set aside.

In a medium mixing bowl, combine the milk and pudding mix. Whisk to blend. Pour into the ramekins or bowls. Dollop ½ teaspoon preserves on top of each. Cover with plastic wrap. Refrigerate for at least 1 hour or up to 3 days.

Makes 4 servings

Per serving: 145 calories, 6 g protein, 30 g carbohydrates, less than 1 g fat (trace saturated), 2 mg cholesterol, 2 g fiber, 357 mg sodium

SETH WORD

Don't be afraid to go to the gym because you are overweight. Nobody cares. And if you don't go to the gym, you'll continue being overweight. Push to get past your fear.

RASPBERRY LEMONADE MOSAICS

When you're tired of the same old gelatin dessert, this is a great, fun alternative. It punches a lot of flavor and is low in . . . well, everything—even for a big serving. It even looks pretty cool. Plus, it doesn't hurt that gelatin is great for joint recovery, which will support your workouts.

2   cups cold water

1   box (4 packets weighing 1 ounce total) unflavored gelatin

2   cups boiling water

1   tub (.3 ounce) Crystal Light Raspberry Lemonade Sugar Free Mix

1   tub (.3 ounce) Crystal Light Lemonade Sugar Free Mix

4   tablespoons aerosol fat-free whipped topping (optional)

4   raspberries (optional)

In a large mixing bowl, combine the cold water with the gelatin. Let stand for 2 minutes. Stir, then add the boiling water. Whisk until the gelatin is completely dissolved. Pour half of the mixture into each of two 8" x 8" glass baking dishes. Add the raspberry lemonade mix to one dish. Whisk to dissolve. Add the lemonade mix to the remaining dish. Whisk to dissolve. Let stand for 15 minutes to cool.

Cover both dishes with plastic wrap. Refrigerate for about 5 hours, or until firm.

Cut each dish of gelatin into 1" cubes. Arrange alternate layers of lemonade and raspberry lemonade cubes in each of 4 martini or white wine glasses. Top each with 1 tablespoon whipped topping and a raspberry, if desired. Serve immediately or cover with plastic wrap and refrigerate for up to 3 days.

Makes 4 servings

Per serving: **43 calories, 6 g protein, 0 g carbohydrates, 0 fat, 0 mg cholesterol, 0 mg fiber, 14 mg sodium**

PUMPKIN-WALNUT SNACK MUFFINS

I've always been one to finish everything I start. When it comes to work, it's great. When it comes to food, well . . . Because I truly believe with all of my being that it's more satisfying to eat a whole muffin (even if it's small) than a half of a muffin (even if it's big), I purposefully made these small. If you need a small treat or a sweet bite to follow an omelet at breakfast, have one. If a major craving hits, splurge and have two. Since they're less than 75 calories each, you can afford to!

I Can't Believe It's Not
Butter! spray

1½ cups whole-grain oat flour

1 teaspoon pumpkin pie
spice

½ teaspoon ground
cinnamon

½ teaspoon baking soda

½ teaspoon baking powder

½ teaspoon salt

½ cup fat-free artificially
sweetened vanilla yogurt

3 large egg whites

½ cup granular sugar
substitute such as Splenda
No Calorie Sweetener,
Granular

1 cup canned pumpkin

2 tablespoon finely chopped
walnuts

Preheat the oven to 350°F. Mist the cups of a standard nonstick muffin pan with I Can't Believe It's Not Butter! spray. Set aside.

In the bowl of a food processor fitted with the metal blade, process the flour for about 1 minute until no coarse grains remain. In a mixing bowl, combine the flour, pumpkin pie spice, cinnamon, baking soda, baking powder, and salt. Sift the mixture twice. Set aside.

In a large mixing bowl, combine the yogurt and egg whites. With a sturdy whisk, beat until thoroughly blended. Add the sugar substitute and the pumpkin. Whisk to blend. Add the reserved flour mixture, stirring, until no flour is visible. Spoon the batter into the prepared cups until each cup is about two-thirds full. Sprinkle on the walnuts.

Bake for 25 to 30 minutes, or until a toothpick inserted into the center of one muffin comes out dry. Cool in the pan on a rack for 10 minutes. Transfer the muffins to the rack. Serve warm or cooled.

Makes 12 muffins

Per muffin: 72 calories, 3 g protein, 11 g carbohydrates, 2 g fat (trace saturated), trace cholesterol, 2 g fiber, 193 mg sodium

Store any leftover muffins in an airtight container in the refrigerator for up to 3 days or freezer for up to 1 month.

SUZY'S JAMMIN' TORTILLAS

Suzy Preston loves this "very good snack" that she created one night when a sweet craving hit. Though it has a bit more natural sugar, you can also use 100% fruit spread instead of sugar-free jelly. Either way, though, it's a treat. For a change of pace, try substituting blackberry, grape, or another favorite flavor for the strawberry preserves.

I Can't Believe It's Not Butter! spray

1 **whole-wheat flour, low-carb tortilla (7½" diameter)**

1 **tablespoon sugar-free strawberry preserves**

Lightly mist a medium nonstick skillet with I Can't Believe It's Not Butter! spray. Set over medium-high heat until it is hot enough for a spritz of water to sizzle on it. Place the tortilla in the pan. Cook for about 3 minutes on each side, or until crisp.

Place the tortilla on a plate. Spritz 6 times with I Can't Believe It's Not Butter! spray. Spread on the jelly. Serve immediately.

Makes 1 serving

Per serving: 80 calories, 4 g protein, 12 g carbohydrates, 3 g fat (less than 1 g saturated), 0 mg cholesterol, 3 g fiber, 260 mg sodium

LISA'S FROZEN GRAMWICHES

This extremely simple snack has become one of Lisa Andreone's favorites. These treats should be stored in an airtight plastic container for up to one month. Remember, because of the high sugar content, it's probably not best to eat this every day, but it certainly does satisfy the occasional craving.

2 whole low-fat graham crackers

¼ cup light or fat-free frozen whipped topping (any flavor)

Break each graham cracker in half to get 4 squares. Spread 2 of the squares evenly with the whipped topping. Top with the remaining squares to make 2 sandwiches. Transfer to a freezer-safe airtight plastic container. Cover tightly and place in the freezer. Freeze for at least 2 hours or up to 1 month. Serve frozen.

Makes 1 serving

Per serving: **150 calories, 2 g protein, 28 g carbohydrates, 4 g fat (2 g saturated), 0 mg cholesterol, less than 1 g fiber, 150 mg sodium**

RASHA AND EDWIN'S WARM GRAPEFRUIT DESSERT

Rasha and Edwin Chapman "like to turn their fruit into dessert." Warming fruit and adding cinnamon, particularly on cold winter nights and mornings, replaces their need for sugar. This simple yet surprisingly delicious treat might soon become a favorite in your house, too—especially in the winter months when grapefruit is at its peak.

1 large grapefruit

1 teaspoon ground
   cinnamon, or to taste

Preheat the oven to 400°F.

Cut the grapefruit in half through the middle. With a serrated citrus knife, loosen the segments, being careful not to cut through the peel. Place the halves, side by side, with the sections facing up, on a baking sheet. Sprinkle with the cinnamon. Bake for 20 minutes, or until warmed through and starting to brown on top. Transfer to serving plates. Let stand for about 5 minutes to cool slightly before serving.

Makes 2 servings

Per serving: 56 calories, 1 g protein, 14 g carbohydrates, trace fat (trace saturated), 0 mg cholesterol, 2 g fiber, trace sodium

CHOCOLATE-KAHLÚA MOUSSE PARFAITS

These parfaits are great when you want to entertain, yet still want to stick to your healthy way of life. Because of the sugar in the graham crackers and whipped topping, however, it's best not to make this an everyday treat. The layered combination of mousse, whipped topping, and graham cracker definitely makes this worth a splurge. I like to serve these desserts in wine glasses for a gorgeous presentation.

½ cup plus 1 tablespoon very cold fat-free milk

¼ cup Kahlúa or other coffee-flavored liqueur

1 envelope (1.5 ounces) sugar-free, low-fat chocolate mousse mix

1 tablespoon unsweetened cocoa powder

2 chocolate graham crackers, crushed into fine crumbs

1 cup thawed fat-free frozen whipped topping

In a large mixing bowl, combine the milk, Kahlúa, mousse mix, and cocoa. With an electric mixer fitted with beaters, whip on low speed until blended. Slowly increase the mixer speed to high, whipping for 5 minutes, or until fluffy.

In each of 4 large wine glasses or glass dessert bowls, layer ¼ cup of the mousse, 2 teaspoons of crumbs, and 2 tablespoons of topping. Repeat layering once more, using the remaining ingredients except for about ⅛ teaspoon of graham cracker crumbs. Sprinkle the top of each serving with a few of the remaining graham cracker crumbs. Refrigerate for at least 2 hours before serving.

Makes 4 servings

Per serving: **145 calories, 3 g protein, 22 g carbohydrates, 3 g fat (2 g saturated), less than 1 mg cholesterol, 1 g fiber, 43 mg sodium**

TIFFANY'S CANDIED ALMONDS

Tiffany Hernandez used to turn to doughnut holes from the Donut Palace. They gave her comfort, she says, "and were particularly excellent when I was feeling overwhelmed with school or house-work." Now, she gets her sweet fix by indulging in this more natural snack that she's sweetened. Though it does have 7 grams of fat, it is mostly heart-healthy fat. Just be careful: I always say that although foods like salmon, avocado, nuts, and seeds are great for your heart, they're not so great for your hips if you overindulge.

I Can't Believe It's Not Butter! spray

1 **ounce whole raw almonds (about 20 almonds)**

1 **teaspoon ground cinnamon**

1 **packet (.035 ounce) sugar substitute (such as Splenda)**

Preheat the oven to 350°F.

Place the almonds in a single layer on a nonstick baking sheet. Bake for 7 to 10 minutes, or until the insides are light brown (test by cutting one nut in half).

Transfer the nuts to a small bowl. Spritz 5 times with I Can't Believe It's Not Butter! spray. Stir. Spritz another 5 times with the spray. Add the cinnamon and sugar substitute. Stir. Spritz 5 times with the spray. Stir. Spritz 5 times with the spray. Stir until as evenly coated as possible (not all of the cinnamon will stick, and you should have spritzed the almonds a total of 20 times, stirring 4 times). Let stand for about 5 minutes to cool and then serve immediately.

Makes 2 servings

Per serving: 88 calories, 3 g protein, 4 g carbohydrates, 7 g fat
(less than 1 g saturated), 0 mg cholesterol, 2 g fiber, 150 mg sodium

Contributors

Chef Devin Alexander, author of *Fast Food Fix,* specializes in creating delicious, flavorful, low-fat makeovers of many popular foods. She has shared her recipes with television audiences on *The Biggest Loser, Good Morning America, The View,* HGTV's *Smart Solutions,* Discovery Health's *National Body Challenge,* and more. Her recipes have also appeared in numerous publications, including *Prevention, Shape, Men's Fitness, Men's Health,* and *Women's Health,* where she is a contributing food editor. She lives in Los Angeles.

Bob Harper, trainer on *The Biggest Loser,* has traveled the world, empowering millions and sharing his successful holistic approach to fitness and weight loss. He is working on a program entitled *Diabetes & You: Step It Up to Get It Down—6.5 Steps Toward Better Blood Sugar Control* to help people with type 2 diabetes control their blood sugar levels. His favorite activities include yoga, running, photography, and reading. According to Bob, the key to life is to realize that today is the first day of the rest of your life—and that you have the power to change anything you put your mind to. He lives in Los Angeles.

Karen Kaplan is an accomplished food and travel writer and editor. She has a Grand Diplome from La Varenne Ecole de Cuisine in Paris, France. A restaurant critic for newspaper and radio for 13 years and an editor, writer, and recipe developer for *Bon Appétit* for 20 years, Karen is also the author of *The Thermador Oven Cookbook*. She lives in Studio City, California.

Kim Lyons, trainer on *The Biggest Loser,* has been physically active her whole life. A graduate of Colorado State University and the National Academy of Sports Medicine, Kim is also an accomplished writer and has been featured in numerous magazines, including *Oxygen, Muscle and Fitness,* and *Self.* When she is not traveling or training, Kim enjoys cooking, studying interior design, and participating in adventure sports. She lives in Hermosa Beach, California.

Acknowledgments

I've compared writing my first cookbook, *Fast Food Fix,* to having a baby. Not only did it take 9 long months, but the radio interviews that followed had me getting up every few hours in the middle of the night. In the end, though, there are few things that have gotten me as excited. This book was like having a baby at record speed, and if it weren't for the incredible team of people who guided and assisted me, it would never have been possible. Thanks to Amy Super who worked with me day to day and quickly proved she is a true rock star. To Chad Bennett who graciously fielded my every phone call and efficiently connected me with contestants, executives, and experts.

To the team at Rodale, most notably Margot Schupf, Erica Gruen, Tina Johnson, Steve Murphy, and Ben Roter, who have presented me with numerous opportunities and have consistently recognized and supported my vision. To Chris Gaugler and Mitch Mandel for the amazing job they did with the food photography. And thanks also to Diane Vezza, the food stylist, and Barb Fritz, the prop stylist.

To the producers and executives of *The Biggest Loser,* particularly Mark Koops, EVP Creative Affairs of Reveille, Dave Broome from 25/7 Productions, Cindy Chang at NBC Universal, and J. D. Roth at 3Ball Productions, who made me the happiest girl ever when they invited me into *The Biggest Loser* family. To Kim Niemi and Neysa Gordon from NBC Universal and Yong Yam from 25/7 Productions, all of whom were integral throughout the process. To my attorney, Matt Krimmer, who totally gets me and keeps me on course.

To *The Biggest Loser* cast and experts who worked with me to translate their recipes to the page exactly as they created them. And for sharing their cravings that inspired some of my own creations.

To *The Biggest Loser* superstar trainers Bob Harper and Kim Lyons, for embracing me and my work, and to Karen Kaplan for writing the chapter introductions and gathering "snapshots" of life on the ranch.

To Heather Haque, who assisted with recipe testing, and Marjorie Clifton, who was integral in developing a handful of dishes.

And a very special thanks to my assistants, Stephanie Farrell and Alexandra Gudmundsson, who are an utter joy to work with and who definitely make my life easier.

Index

Underscored page references indicate boxed text or tips. **Boldfaced** page references indicate photographs.

Water
   before and after meal, 100
   in Biggest Loser diet, 4–5
   water weight gain, 62
Water chestnuts
   Asian Meatball Soup, 114–15,
      115
   Kimmi and Bruce's Chicken
      Lettuce Wraps, 78–79, **79**
   Spinach Skinny-Dip, 84
Weight-loss tips
   alcoholic beverages, 196
   carbohydrates, 32, 59
   cardio workouts, 83
   chocolate snacks, 205
   counting calories, 111, 180
   drinking water, 100
   eating out, 152, 159, 182
   exercise, 104
   fruit, 142
   getting back to diet, 5, 206
   getting rid of unhealthy food,
      130
   grocery shopping, 44
   gyms and health clubs, 72, 203

mental attitude, 35
modifying recipes, 80, 122
muscle weight, 62
photographs on refrigerator, 43
protein, 59
restrictive diets, 191
stocking kitchen with healthy
   food, 130
strength training, 203
vegetables, 59, 142
water weight, 62
whole foods, choosing, 135
Wilcox, Kelly, 28
Wine, 5
Wolff, Marty, 25, 199
Word, Seth, 18, 47, 206
Wraps. *See* Rollups and wraps
Wylie, Mark, 25, 113

Y

Yesitis, Mark, 21–22, 46
Yoga, 11

Yogurt
   Blackberry Sorbet–Filled
      Lemon Cups, 200,
      201
   Boston-Cream Peanut-Butter
      Breakfast Banana Split, 32,
      33
   Chocolate-Cherry Breakfast
      Smoothie, 36, **36**
   Marty's Creamy Pineapple
      Sorbet, 199
   One-Serving Chocolate
      Cheesecakes, 197
   Suzanne's Cinnamon-Apple
      Breakfast Pockets,
      58

Z

Zucchini
   Big Rooby's Almost-Famous
      Skillet Fajitas, 172

THE BIGGEST LOSER: THE WORKOUT DVD

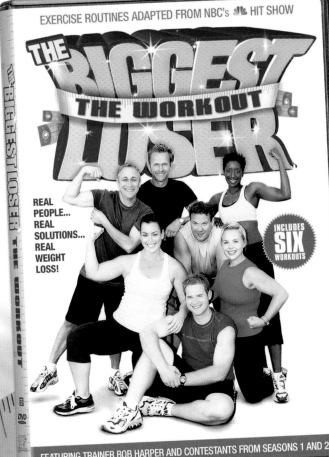

EXERCISE ROUTINES ADAPTED FROM NBC's HIT SHOW

THE **BIGGEST** THE WORKOUT **LOSER**

REAL PEOPLE... REAL SOLUTIONS... REAL WEIGHT LOSS!

INCLUDES **SIX** WORKOUTS

FEATURING TRAINER BOB HARPER AND CONTESTANTS FROM SEASONS 1 AND 2

SHED THE POUNDS!

Real People...
Real Solutions...
Real Results!

Available Now!

47 48 50

37

Step It Up!

THE BIGGEST LOSER
THE WORKOUT 2

On DVD in December!

SERIOUS ABOUT LOSING WEIGHT?
JOIN THE CLUB!

THE BIGGEST LOSER CLUB

Try the Web's most complete weight loss program today!

Why take your weight loss and healthy living goals online with The Biggest Loser Club? For starters, you'll find: Hundreds of additional recipes ■ Tips and feedback from the trainers and show contestants ■ Support from our team of experts and other members ■ Customized meal plans, suited to your tastes ■ Tools to keep you on track toward your calorie targets ■ Automatic shopping lists ■ Individualized exercise plans based on your fitness level and goals ■ Convenient 24/7 access

NBC

Go online TODAY for your FREE diet profile!
Visit www.biggestloserclub.com/cookbook

200722401